Making

Secrets Of Happy Couples Nobody Tells You About

By

Nicolas Kelton

Table of Contents

Chapter 4: Communicating Love Effectively To Your Partner

Introduction

The twenty-first-century couple is surrounded by a web of demands associated with a seemingly continuously advancing world. Having to juggle a full-time job, career pursuit, and the commitments of a serious love relationship/family, it can become indeed overwhelming. We are continuously faced with the big challenge of how to create a love that can stand through the test of time. How do we find the right balance between our relationship, career and the one million other commitments that we are tied to while still living our very best lives?

A lot of my friends and I have found ourselves caught deeply in this web as well – coming to a point where it seemed like our relationships were literally slipping out of our fingers and we became so unsure of how to redeem the situation. We thought we were giving it our best, but alas our best wasn't good enough. We have sought answers in psychologists and relationship experts who have had so many things to tell us and have recommended volumes of books for us to read, which we barely have time for.

In desperate need to find workable and practical answers to the lasting love I craved, I began to research and practice realistic approaches that have turned my relationship and that of my friends' around in such a short time. This book is a culmination of answers to perhaps the biggest challenge that present-day couples face – "how do we create and sustain a lasting love?" It will first help you understand why it seems like love fades away over time and why that's not your fault. You will go further to see practical realistic approaches to understanding how to communicate love effectively and how to grow and sustain a healthy love life amidst your very busy lives.

You will learn great communication and conflict resolution strategies, which are easy to follow and are guaranteed to yield awesome results. I have tried out most of the strategies written in this book and I have invited many of my friends to try them out. As a result, we have all had tremendous outcomes, so believe me when I say it is not that hard to follow and it works – you just have to be as intentional and determined as I was and soon you too will recover those beautiful moments when it seemed like you couldn't take your eyes off your partner for a second. But the time to start doing something to create the change you want is now, not tomorrow, and the fact that you are looking up resources shows that you have taken a good first step towards creating a love that lasts.

Hopefully, you can read through this book in just a few hours and get to work on your amazing relationship. Know that it is worth it, and you are worth all the happiness in the world too.

Chapter 1: When Love Seems To Have Changed Over Time

Many people have asked: "Why don't I feel the butterflies anymore when I look at my partner?" "Why don't I get the shivers I used to get by just thinking of him/her?" "Is the connection lost between us?" "What's happening to the romance between us?" These and many more are amongst the questions many couples in long-standing relationships have encountered at some point or another if they are honest with themselves. Those in newer relationships would encounter questions like these too in just a matter of time.

So, does love really change between two individuals after a while? The answer is - Yes it does! Do you often imagine why a lot of couples that had such a powerful romantic connection suddenly feel like they have fallen out of love or are no longer meant for each other? Some of the reasons can be linked to not understanding what happens to a romantic love over time. Working with these dynamics can help sustain a healthier and lasting relationship.

Let us first try to understand some science relating to the "love" feeling. The brain is the wonderful organ that is responsible for interpreting the feeling of "love" as well as so many other feelings. One renowned scientist, Dr. Helen Fisher, spent many years discovering that when we feel a strong attraction towards another person, what actually happens is that the brain releases chemicals like dopamine in large amounts, which gives us the "feel good" sensation. It plants and grows the desire to always be with that person and to think about them all the time.

At this point, the tendency is that we might not even see the person's faults, or we might see the faults but simply overlook them because of this feeling that has consumed us. We see the person as perfect for us and all we want to do is be by their side all the time. We are convinced we want to be with this person forever. This is the period when we believe we have "fallen in love" [19].

Scientists like Fisher also believe that the evolutionary reason for this strong attraction is the sole purpose of mating and reproduction and that is why sexual attraction is imminent when you first fall in love. The hormones testosterone and estrogen are very active at this point. [19, 33] This is the point whereby many couples decide that they are meant for each other and want to ensure a lasting love by committing to marriage or a legal partnership in order to forever secure this "'love" that they have for each other.

But here's the shocker – Fisher's research and those of Psychologists Dorothy Tennov and John Money have proven that this mating phase is naturally designed to last only a few months, at most a few years, after which the surge of hormones begins to dwindle and reality sets in [19, 26, 33].

The high rush of the "feel good" chemicals the brain releases begin to normalize, and the butterflies begin to disappear. [19] It is usually at this phase that a lot of relationships begin to have problems. People suddenly start to acknowledge each other's faults, even though these faults have been staring them in the face the whole time. Many relationships could hit the rocks at this point.

For example, research conducted in the US showed that the peak of divorces is seen between year five to year seven of marriages [2]. Researchers have suggested that the disappearance of this "feel good" sensation might be a strong reason why most divorces occur after the first few years of marriage [19]. Once these chemicals have worn off, it appears that the scales have fallen off your eyes and the statement – "love is blind" ceases to suffice.

Couples at this stage try to find the feelings they first had when they started off but are unable to resurrect those feelings, so they decide that they might no longer be in love or even compatible and that they might be better off going their separate ways.

So, what happens when reality finally kicks in? Don't get it wrong! This is not a bad thing and a lot of couples enjoy a healthy loving and lasting relationship. Harvard medical school professors, Richard Schwartz and Jacqueline Olds, say love at this stage is believed to have evolved to a much deeper and lasting feeling that is no longer based on butterflies in one's tummy or the surge of hormones.

It becomes a softer feeling – a warmth that fills you up and is even more satisfying. It brings comfort and it is constant [30]. Our emotions begin to readjust to a more sincere and earnest feeling of love in our relationship. This love will now be based on genuine intimacy, common values, and faith in each other. Also, it will be based on mutual respect and a determination to go into the future together.

It is true that you begin to see each other's faults, but you also learn to forgive them and become more tolerant of them – accepting each other the way you are with imperfections and all. Both of you are now probably able to find a safe place in each other as well. This is true love and it lasts even without the butterflies. Real love is more than just the excitement you feel gazing at your partner while losing track of time.

It's more than the distraction your partner brings while you are trying so hard to concentrate at work. It is more than all the physical attractions and pulse-raging feelings that seem to want to explode your heart. All these intense feelings would calm down as time goes on, giving birth to a more subtle kind of love that can withstand the test of time.

The contrast with the early stage of falling in love is that in this later stage, you could perceive your love to be less exciting or even boring. You should learn to nurture and appreciate what you have at this point and not make the mistake of comparing it to what you had at first like a lot of couples do. If you do this, you would be setting your relationship up for a lot of disappointment and dissatisfaction. This, in turn, can kill whatever love is left between you and a breakup becomes imminent.

So again, does love really change over time? Yes, love continues to evolve in a relationship, but if armed with the right tools, love can evolve into such a formidable force that it becomes somewhat unbreakable.

Chapter 2: Use It Or Lose It - Why You Constantly Have To Work On Your Relationship

Relationships are hard work and therefore, only for the mature and serious-minded. If you want one, then both you and your intended partner have to prepare to do the work to keep it thriving or else you just might lose it. Imagine how you have to work on maintaining your car – fuelling it regularly, washing it and servicing it so it can serve you optimally. You also check the tires for wear and pay attention to any fault signals the car may be showing you. What happens if you continuously ignore those signals? One day you won't have a car to drive anymore. We know this about our vehicles, so we put in the effort.

Consider your living space as well; I bet we put in some effort as well in maintaining where we live by cleaning up the floors, washing dishes, doing the laundry, and so on. The effort we put into our space, in turn, makes our lives more comfortable. What if your home is left unkempt for weeks or months? Unwashed dishes and left-over food lying around the place. Roaches and rodents might even be your guests. Gradually, as the house is left without care, your once beautiful and comfortable space becomes unhealthy and uncomfortable. Some serious work would have to be put in to reverse the situation even though it could have been totally avoided if the little bits of everyday effort were put in place.

Think of a relationship with these two illustrations in mind. A once-loving and safe relationship can also turn out to be unbearable, uncomfortable, and even toxic if both parties do not put in the work that is involved in nurturing and maintaining a healthy relationship.

Unfortunately, it is especially more challenging in this era of modern romance to work at a relationship constantly and consistently. People are becoming busier, taking on more and more responsibilities daily

(13, 17, 24). The physical and mental demands of a full-time job, a demanding business, or education have continuously been on the rise, and we have to combine all of these factors and maybe more with upholding a relationship. A lot of times, it is the relationship that gradually starts to suffer cuts in attention and some neglect which can, in turn, lead to problems cropping up.

We can find a way to give our relationships the work and attention that it needs despite our busy lives. Simply put, if you don't take out the time and pay the sacrifice to work on your relationship now, it could slip through your fingers before you even realize it. Remind yourself of how and why you built up your relationship in the first place - maybe that can inspire you to start putting in some good effort into nurturing it. If that doesn't inspire you, then some of these other important reasons just might motivate you.

Reasons Why You Should Work On Your Relationship

- **You should work on your relationship because it is worth it:**

  Do you value your partner? Have you had great times with this person and are convinced that what you have is special? Do you believe that this is what both of you want for your lives? If you agree that both of you are deserving of each other and the relationship that you share, then you also would agree that the relationship is worth putting in the work to help it grow and thrive. Remember, where your treasure is, there also your heart will be.

- **You should work on your relationship so you can survive a possible "storm":**

  Constantly working on a relationship will continue to strengthen both of you and what you have for each other. Putting in the conscious effort into communication, spending time together, working on intimacy, doing things for each other, giving compliments and gifts and so on will someday pay off greatly. A time will come when the strength of your relationship will be tested. It might be a financial issue or an issue with family or friends or perhaps a big change that no one was prepared for, like sickness or losing your job. We do not wish for these things and no one wants to land on a rocky road unprepared, but what if it happens? Will you be ready for it? Will your relationship survive an impact? If you work together now to continuously build and nurture a healthy relationship, then hopefully the relationship might come out stronger and both parties unscarred.

- **You should work on your relationship so you can both enjoy a smooth-running journey:**

Just like the car illustration, constantly working on your relationship sets the stage for a smooth-sailing experience with each other. For example, if you make conscious effort to improve your listening skills with your partner, then you can better understand their needs and it could save you a fight or two in the future that could result from an issue they tried to talk to you about but you didn't quite pay attention. It's the simple things like that we could work on and it could make a dramatic improvement to our experience with our partner. When the relationship is a happy and safe space for both parties, you become happier and more productive in your life in general. So, listen to the signs now and do the work to get your relationship to where you want it to be. Perhaps you need to work on your communication skills or giving compliments or intimacy. Whatever it is, don't wait until things get worse. Ever heard of the saying "a stitch in time saves nine"? It might be easier to make these changes at an earlier onset of a problem than at a later stage. So start working now!

- **The initial intense sparks you had may die off soon:**

Everyone knows that when you first enter a relationship, you are so in love and crazy about each other. This is the initial surge of emotions you feel that could even cloud your thinking [19, 33]. Both of you try so hard and consciously to please each other and you tend to overlook a lot of your partner's mistakes. Then gradually, when the love chemicals in the brain have normalized, you begin to find issues with matters that you would normally ignore. That is why it is so important to work on all the factors that would build and strengthen your relationship right from the start. Do not ignore those signs now; instead, talk about them, helping each other to grow into the man/woman that you can always love. When it eventually seems like the bold sparks have calmed down, it becomes easier to keep a warm glowing fire of love burning that had been built and strengthened by all the work both of you have put, and continually put, into the relationship.

- **You should work on your relationship continuously so you can get the best out of both yourself and your partner:**

Perhaps we should illustrate this time using our

own bodies – when we take care of our bodies adequately, we get the maximum use out of them. To do this, we need to eat right, sleep right, exercise, and so on. This helps us live healthier and happier and in turn, we are able to go about our lives and perform our activities to the fullest. The same applies to our relationships – when a person feels genuinely loved, satisfied, and attended to, then I would imagine they can generally be happier and content. And what is more beautiful than living with a happy partner? If your relationship brings out the best in you, then you should never stop putting in the effort that in turn, makes you happy and fulfilled; if you doubt that your relationship brings out the best in you, then maybe it's time to consciously do some work on it and, who knows, eventually your potentials will start to shine through.

- **You should work on your relationship continuously because you love each other:**
Ever heard of the phrase "love is worth fighting

for"? What brought both of you together in the first place? Was it genuine love? Then it is worth working hard for. So, if you love your partner and wouldn't want to lose them, this is the primary, and probably most important reason, why we must work on our relationships constantly. Love is not enough – it has to be accompanied by a conscious and mutual effort by both parties.

Remember that two consenting and committed adults must be involved in the continuous care and nurturing of any successful relationship, both giving to each other, resulting in a formidable connection that is mutually beneficial.

Finding The Balance Between Your Relationship And Other Factors In Your Life

In case you have already been properly motivated as to why you have to put in some good effort into making your relationship grow and bloom, but you are still faced with the challenge of a very busy life and you are unsure where to make the adjustments to properly fit in your relationship, perhaps some of these tips might guide you.

Keep in mind though that having a serious relationship does not imply that your career or business has to suffer a fall. In fact, research has proven that happy people tend to reach higher career goals, make more money, live healthier, and excel more generally than single people [9]. Yes, it might involve some sacrifice on your part, but then what use is all the effort you make in your life if you still feel empty, unloved, and unhappy? When your emotional needs are properly met in a happy and loving relationship, then the likelihood is that you can go out there to face your responsibilities and all the challenges of your life knowing that you are genuinely loved and cherished by someone you share the same feelings with.

- **Talk about it:**

As we know by now, communication is the fuel of any relationship, so talk. Talk about your job/commitments with your partner and how demanding it is getting. Let them know, for example, that you are pursuing a new project and in the coming months, it might take up a lot of your time. Let them know that you are thinking about them always and the project does not take their place. Tell them ahead of time as well so they can be mentally prepared. The same applies to when you have to work weekends or put in some extra hours or are being held down by your boss. Talk to your partner and update them as things change. Hopefully, they can understand.

- **Get your priorities right:**

This is not to say you have to decide who gets more of your attention – your career or your relationship. Of course, you need to earn a living and you want a loving partner as well. Prioritizing doesn't mean that one aspect has to suffer. It means at every one time, you need to know where to pay more attention. For instance, your partner is going through a hard time emotionally because they lost a loved one. This means they need you more at that period and that is not the time to take up extra hours at the office or new engagements. Again, perhaps you have a big presentation coming up in two days and you really need to work hard at it. Then it may not be the time to book a dinner outing; except, of course, if you feel you can combine both commitments. Let your partner know why you have to focus on work for that period of time and find other ways of keeping the connection going.

- **Make up for any lost time as soon as you can:**

  As patient and understanding as your partner is, don't push too hard with them. When you know you have been so busy with other commitments recently, become conscious of making it up to them. Try to make up for the time you couldn't be with them as soon as you can.

- **Maximize the free time:**

Make great use of the holidays and weekends and days off. Plan ahead to do interesting things with your partner so that by the time you get busy again, they would have gotten a good amount of your time and attention.

- **Have a large heart:**

Remember that you have someone else in your life now, so you have to be accommodating. Learn to apologize instead of arguing aimlessly. You should learn to forgive easily as well. You know your partner loves you so stop counting how many times they came home late or forgot to call. Expand your capacity to let go of little issues easily.

- **Be supportive:**

Let your partner know that you support their career goals and dreams and that you will be there for them. Chances are, when they can see that you truly support them, they will extend that support to you and your career/commitments as well. Remember, you can't expect what you don't give.

- **Make time for each other:**

Since you claim to love your partner and you have committed yourself to a relationship with them, then you have to make out time for them. Who works 24 hours a day, 7 days a week, and 30 days a month? Even if you do, it is high time you start to give your relationship a portion of that time. Planning ahead always works here as you can plan your calendar with your partner in mind. Making out time might also require some sacrifice, but then is there love without some amount of sacrifice? Meet up somewhere for lunch in the middle of the day if that is possible, give up your scheduled hang out with colleagues sometimes, take a day off work to be with them. If you are really bent on fostering a serious healthy relationship, then you will consciously find the time.

- **Keep communication going throughout the day:**

Try to communicate when you get the chance at work. Short calls, chats and text messages work greatly. It shows your partner that you have them in mind even though you are busy working.

- **Don't mix work and relationship time together:**

As much as you can, try not to bring up work when you have set out time to be with your partner. It is not the time to reply to work emails and take work calls except when you absolutely have to. When you say you are spending time with them, then really be present. Give them your full, uninterrupted attention.

Chapter 3: Asking Questions – A Powerful Communication Tool

It is common knowledge that a successful relationship requires great communication. We can never overemphasize the importance of talking to each other in a relationship, as it is a great way to sustain an intimate connection, tackle conflicts, and plan the future in general. A couple should be able to share ideas and to openly communicate about targets, fears, conflicts, and dreams.

With all the emphasis on communication, this important factor still poses as one of the major areas couples are failing daily. There is simply not enough communication going on in many relationships, unfortunately. Some couples can't talk about their sex lives even when it is clear they are having big issues. They perceive that aspect to be a talking taboo or a somewhat 'no-go' area. This can gradually kill their relationship because of the onset and increase of dissatisfaction and disappointments in that regard.

There are different kinds of people in terms of communication. While some have absolutely no problem talking about and communicating their thoughts, others may be introverted or shy and communication can require such great effort from them. Other reasons why couples can have issues communicating include:

- **A desire to please a partner:**

  This happens especially in a new relationship. You want to say and do all the right things. You might also be unsure as to how your partner will respond or feel with regards to certain questions, so you simply don't ask them, but then you don't get to know the answers too. This could cause some friction in the future.

- **Religious/cultural/family background:**

  Different cultures and religions might have different approaches to relationships. Some people have come from families where they saw one parent always quiet and never asking the questions. Others have a religious background that teaches submission from one partner, especially in marriage. These people enter relationships later in life with these background ideas and it may affect their openness to questioning their partner simply because they might think they would be disrespectful or too bold. Some cultural backgrounds also have issues like sex as sacred and never discussed and as a result, the individual can find it strange in a relationship where the partner wants to talk about sex.

- **Psychological disposition:**

Past experiences like a previous bad relationship can affect an individual's orientation to communication and the act of asking questions in a relationship. For example, if in a previous relationship, one partner wasn't the talking type and was not open to answering questions and communication in general, this could affect the partner's orientation to asking questions in a new relationship, as they might not expect the new partner to answer questions easily too; therefore, it is possible that they begin to hold back some pressing questions.

No matter the reason why communication seems to be an issue for a couple, there are great strategies to help understand each other and get along better. One of these communication pillars is **the practice of asking questions** [7]. Whether you are in a new relationship or have been together for ages, the practice of asking questions is pivotal to getting to really know your partner. It might seem like such a simple thing – just asking a question, right? But asking the right questions can make a big difference in building a strong relationship and gaining the trust of your partner.

Psychologist, Dr. Lonnie Barbach tells us "Questions give people the skill and direction to talk about things constructively" and that is so true [8]. She also goes on to say that at the beginning of a relationship, most couples are moved to do what they think would please each other, but guess what - it is only a guessing game if you don't ask the questions and most people are bad guessers [8]. Isn't it easier to just ask the questions and take away the anxiety of wondering whether you have pleased a partner or not rather than just making the assumptions? If you agree, then we can say that asking questions, to a large extent, clears up doubts and confusion.

Benefits Of Asking Question I: Getting To Really Know Your Partner

Asking questions, especially the right questions, are very important in getting to know your partner, even more so if you are in a new relationship or still considering entering one. "It is not just about finding out if you are compatible but more about knowing your differences and understanding them so you can accept them", says Barbach of the popular happy couples' app [8]. No matter how you perceive the question might sound, it is better to ask it and to be at rest than to live wondering what the answer might be. You don't automatically know a person's favourite colour or food from the start - you have to ask it!

In summary, here are some important benefits of asking questions on the journey to really getting to know your partner:

- To ensure you are both on the same page
- To set your mind at ease
- To clarify confusions and doubts
- To help you understand your partner's emotional needs
- To enable you to understand your partner's goals and dreams
- To help you better understand your partner's weaknesses
- To help you understand the motives for your partner's actions
- To take care of the guessing games and assumptions

- To know what expectations your partner has from you and from the relationship

Remember, asking the right question at the right time is key to getting the answers you seek to foster a healthier relationship [7].

Here are some random examples of questions you can ask to help you get to know your partner better:

- What are your goals in a relationship?
- Where do you see us in a year's time?
- What's the major way you express your love?
- Is it ok if I have close friends of the opposite sex?
- How do you feel about my exes?
- What would you prefer to do on a Saturday night?
- Is it important for you to divide up chores?
- What is your ideal vacation?
- How important is sex to you?
- How do you feel about the kind of job that I do?
- How's your relationship with your family?

- How would you prefer to deal with a conflict between us?
- What can I do to make you feel loved?
- What does a perfect day look like to you?
- What is your most treasured memory?

Benefits Of Asking Questions II: Building Trust And Intimacy

As important as asking questions is to the beginning of a relationship while you are starting out getting to know each other, it is also very important at all stages after that, especially in forging trust and intimacy between both parties. Trust is very important in any relationship and you can't build a relationship successfully if you can't communicate effectively. If you are going to communicate and understand each other's emotional needs, personal habits, love language, personal boundaries, sex preferences, communication patterns, and goals and dreams, you need to trust each other.

Here are some more tailored examples of questions in various categories that can help a couple build up trust and intimacy in a relationship.

a. Feeling loved:

Everyone has a different way that makes them feel loved. This especially varies between men and women. For example, women tend to be more emotional and men more physical. You shouldn't expect that the way you feel loved is the same way your partner will – you need to ask them and check again with them every once in a while to be sure you are doing it right. You can ask questions like:

- What's the main way you would like for me to show my love?
- How important are compliments to you?
- How often would you want me to say, "I love you"?
- How important are gifts to you?

b. Respect:

Everyone wants to feel like they are respected and treated right, both in private and in the public eye. So, respect is very essential in a relationship. Here are some examples of questions that can help you know how your partner feels about respecting you (and each other) in the relationship.

- How do you feel about the respect I give you?
- Do you feel I respect you enough?
- How do you feel about respecting each other in public?
- How would you like me to show that I respect you?
- How much does respect in a relationship mean to you?

c. Kindness:

To understand your partner's attitude to kindness, you can ask questions like these:

- How do you feel about giving to charity?
- How do you feel about giving to the homeless/poor on the streets?
- What do you think about paying the bus fare for a total stranger?
- What would you say is your limit to kindness?

d. Communication:

As communication is one of the major pillars in a relationship, it is so important to understand the best way your partner communicates their feelings and thoughts to you. Asking them questions to know their communication patterns is key. You can ask questions like these:

- How do you think we can improve our communication?
- What would you say about the amount of time we spend talking?
- What is the best time you would prefer for us to have a serious conversation?

- How do you feel about texting over phone calls when we are apart from each other?
- When would you rather not talk?
- How would you prefer for us to resolve a disagreement/conflict?
- How would you feel if I interrupted you while you are speaking?

e. Emotional needs:

Understanding each other's emotional needs in a relationship will help you to better meet them. Some people tend to be more emotionally expressive while others are experts at bottling up their emotions and it becomes harder to reach them. How to better manage and meet each other's emotional needs can only be fully understood by asking the right questions. So try questions like these:

- How would you like for me to treat you when you are down or feeling depressed?

- Would you rather be left alone when you are angry?
- Do you cry easily?
- What's the best way to cheer you up when you are sad?

f. Personal boundaries:

Boundaries are like peoples' personal fences – where they wouldn't want anyone to cross including their partners. Instead of getting into arguments over boundaries, it is better to know them and understand why they are important to your partner. This in turns helps you to respect and possibly avoid the boundaries so you can enjoy a happy and trust-based relationship. So, if you are trying to learn about your partner's boundaries, you can ask questions like these:

- When will you rather be left alone?
- When wouldn't you want me present?
- How will I know you want some personal space?

- What topic is a no-go area for you?

g. Sex:

There are probably different ways people like to communicate with their partners regarding their sexual lives. There are verbal and non-verbal sex languages. Again, when you are unsure about what your partner wants, it is simply better to ask the question. That way you can understand each other's needs better and can comfortably forge a stronger intimacy. The frustrations and dissatisfactions can also most likely be tackled here, leaving both parties happy and living their best lives.

Some questions you can ask include:

- How often would you like to have sex?
- What's your most preferred sex position?
- When would you rather not have sex?
- What would you say about our current sex life?
- How would you rate my/your kissing?

- Is there anything you would like for me to do better during sex?
- What do you think about exploring new things in our sex life?

h. Personal habits:

Habits are practices that can be hard to give up. Some of them have been built over time and it becomes very difficult to change. Trying to tackle and understand your partner's habits can be hard, especially if you don't agree with them. You can ask important questions tailored to understanding your partner's habits and help them realize how said habit affects you or the relationship. For example, if your partner smokes and you want to talk about this habit, try questions like:

- How do you feel about your smoking?
- How do you feel your smoking/habit affects our relationship?

- Would you be open to seeking help with this habit?
- What if I am not comfortable with 'this' habit, how would that make you feel?

i. Disagreement and Differences:

You can't always agree on everything in a relationship. The conflicts will eventually come. Agreeing ahead of time on how to handle these disagreements will help both of you in the long run. There are several ways out there that relationship experts have suggested can resolve conflicts more effectively. Talk with your partner ahead of time to understand what works better for them. Try asking questions like:

- How would you rather handle fights?
- What do you think should be done when we can't agree on a matter?
- How important is it to you to win an argument?
- How do you feel about accepting blame?

- What do we argue about the most and how can we change that?
- How does our arguing make you feel?
- How can we fix 'this' issue so we don't have to argue about it all the time?
- How do you feel about bringing in a trusted third party to help resolve a conflict?

j. Time together and time apart:

Different people can have different ideas about how much is enough time to spend together and apart. Does your partner feel they are being starved of your time or do they feel you take way too much of their time? Do you need schedules? Do you quarrel about timing? Some of these issues can be resolved by simply asking the right questions. This helps you understand what both of you want with regards to how much time to spend together comfortably. So go ahead and ask some of these questions:

- How do you feel about the amount of time we spend together?
- How frequently do you think we should have sleepovers?
- How often would you want to hang out with your friends instead?
- What do you think about the amount of space we give each other?
- How much alone time do you require?

k. Goals and dreams:

It is important to understand what goals you and your partner have for the relationship. Are you just trying out things? Do you see yourselves headed for something more long term? Do you see the possibility of having children? What if your partner has a completely different idea from yours? At the point you realize this, it could cause big conflicts that can hugely impair or end the relationship all because you failed to have that talk about your goals for your relationship. Understanding your partner's dreams for life is also important and helps you know in time if and how you can fit into the picture. Imagine your partner is big into adventure and dreams of selling off their things one day to begin traveling the world. Is this something you can happily do with them or are you a non-risk taker that prefers to take roots in one place? You simply need to ask these questions since you can't just assume or guess a person's dreams, can you? So try asking questions like:

- Where do you see us in the next year?
- How do you feel about having children?
- If you had your choice, what job would you rather be doing?
- Where do you think our relationship is heading?
- What are your goals in this relationship?
- What do you think should be the next step in our relationship?
- When do you think it is the right time to take the next step in our relationship?
- What goals do you have for yourself financially?

The Secret To Getting The Best Answers To Your Questions: Asking Open-Ended Questions

We have established that asking questions can be such a great way to communicate optimally in relationships [8, 35]. It is also a great way to avoid long, aimless arguments. Both those starting a new relationship and those already in a long-term relationship can benefit from asking questions. However, we have also emphasized that asking the right questions is the key to getting the right answers and hence improving communication with our partners.

But what is the right kind of questions to ask to improve communication between partners?

Psychologists and relationship experts have shown that open-ended questions are the best kind of questions to ask to get a great conversation going [31, 35]. These are questions that do not have a 'yes' or 'no' response. They are statements, which require a response that is usually a conversation style response. These questions are designed to convey much more information than a simple 'yes' or 'no', which does not leave you with much [29, 31].

The quality of the answers you get from your partner has a significant effect on the standard of the relationship. Generally, and a lot of times, the questions we ask are framed by our opinions, judgment, ideas or directives, and are not exactly genuine questions that seek to listen to the other person's opinions or ideas. We are used to expressing our own opinions in terms of our tone of voice and body language. We put out close-ended questions without even realizing it and hugely limit the responses of our partners.

Open-ended questions are great and work better. They invite your partner to a conversation rather than a straightforward one-word answer. This is a different and better kind of experience, but it requires the right skills, which can, of course, be learned. It also requires a good amount of confidence in yourself and a measure of respect and trust for the answers your partner will give. In addition, you have to be open to ideas and opinions that are not yours, so you can't be stuck on your own opinions anymore.

If you are ready to go down this route, open-ended questions would most likely get you open-ended answers, which can become authentic, healthy discussions that let your partner know their experiences are important to you and you are genuinely interested in hearing what they have to say.

For example, when you ask a question like "How do you feel about the amount of time we spend together?", it prompts your partner to say their opinion about the matter. It tells them you are open to listening to what they have to say about the amount of time spent together. It shows a great deal of regard and respect and, most likely, they will speak their mind. The other way that question can be asked is "Do we spend enough time together?" This way, you build up the pressure on them to say a 'yes' or 'no'. Also, it is most likely clear that your opinion is that you don't spend enough time together, leaving your partner with little or no chance to really voice their thoughts, but rather sway them in your direction.

Consider another example: You want to ask your partner's opinion on giving gifts. You could say, "How important are gifts to you?" This question is neutral, open-ended, and opens up the floor for a conversation where you can better understand what your partner thinks about exchanging gifts. Whereas the close-ended version could sound like this: "Are gifts important to you?" This option will not likely get you the best response from your partner and you could end up with a 'yes' or 'no'.

A close-ended question will, in contrast, convey the

wrong message, which will likely say that your own experience is more important than that of your partner [29, 31]. Of course, there are cases where an open-ended question is just a waste of time and totally unnecessary.

For example, if you wanted to know whether your partner wants their coffee with or without milk, you would ask it straight like this: "Do you want your coffee black or with milk?" You wouldn't go saying, "What do you think about drinking your coffee with or without milk?", because it isn't necessary. Another example is asking "Can I get you anything else from the kitchen?" which really requires a simple "no, thanks" or a "yes, please", as opposed to asking an open-ended question like "How do you feel about me getting something else for you from the kitchen?" Again, that might be unnecessary.

Open-ended questions have their limits and are important for building communication, trust, and intimacy. In summary, some of the many benefits of asking open-ended questions include:

- To show your partner your desire to communicate because of your genuine likeness for them
- To get your partner talking and start a great conversation
- To make room for change and synergy of ideas
- To let your partner know that you respect them and their opinions.
- To allow your partner the chance to open up to you and share their thoughts and feelings
- To take the pressure off your partner to reach a quick and abrupt answer

Some other tips to get the best experience from asking questions include:

- **Get your motives right.**

  Before you ask the question, you need to ask yourself if you are simply curious about what your partner has to say, or if it is really about your needs and improving your overall experience.

- **Get ready to talk as well.**

  Remember open-ended questions are an invitation for a discussion. So, when your partner wants your opinion, be ready to give your own views on the subject.

- **Ask focused questions as much as possible.**

  Instead of generalizing a question in a very broad manner, try focusing on what you are really interested in hearing or getting your partner to speak about. For instance, instead of saying "What do you feel about respect in a relationship?", try being more specific by asking, "What do you feel about the amount of respect I give you?"

- **Be an active listener.**

  Become a curious listener. Instead of thinking and piling up what to say in response to your partner, you should actually pay rapt attention, not judging, and be completely in the moment with an aim to understand what your partner is saying. It sounds like a difficult thing to do right? But it has been proven by several pieces of research to work!

- **Timing is Key.**

You know your partner and you know the best time to likely get them talking. If you go to a football lover when they are engrossed in a game and begin to ask open-ended questions, you might not likely get a conversation at that point. Some people won't talk when they are tired or upset or even hungry. Read the signs. You know that partner best!

Chapter 4: Communicating Love Effectively To Your Partner

Why Are We So Different In Behavior?

People differ in many possible ways. Physically, there are all kinds of people – from tall to short, fat to slim, black to white. These are amongst so many other physical differences that make us the unique people that we are. In terms of behavior, we also vary – from the out-going extrovert to the quiet and calm introvert, the soft tempered to the easily tempered, the bold to the shy, the attention seeker to the one who always wants to go unnoticed.

The way we differ depends on a number of factors including sex, geography, genetics, sociology, and cultural/religious and family backgrounds. In the same way, we all have different dispositions regarding love and emotions. Simply put, the way we give and receive love differs just as we are all different. Again, our upbringing and other factors mentioned can influence our different attitudes to love.

For example, if someone was raised in a family where they were used to seeing their parents do things for each other all the time and share love in this manner, they could grow up with this practice instilled in them and later on go on to develop a habit of doing things, like helping out with chores, for their partner. When a partner also reciprocates these acts, it would make them feel loved. This is because that was the emotional language they had grown up accustomed to.

If the case was the giving of gifts regularly by one or both parents and the child grew up watching this expression of love, they could also become hugely influenced by this practice and go on later in life to expect the regular giving of gifts from their partner, and when this is not the case, they might start to feel unloved.

But what if a partner is not moved by gifts and simply expects you to say the words to let them know how you feel? There becomes a problem when the gift giver cannot seem to understand why even with all the gifts, their partner still feels unloved. The gift-giver has to understand the way their partner wants to receive love, which is by means of words, or else this partner might just continue to feel there is no more love in the relationship; if this feeling persists, it could grow into something more catastrophic, like a break-up or divorce.

Therefore, there is a great need to understand how your partner wants you to express your love for them or, as Dr. Gary Chapman, a bestseller author and renowned relationship and marriage counselor, put it – their "love language"[14]. Many factors come into play when the aim is to create a love that lasts between couples. Chapman says, "the need to feel loved is a primary human emotional need" and this is why this subject is so important.

Communication always plays a huge frontline role in

relationships, but how can you communicate effectively if you don't, first of all, understand how your partner responds to the love you are trying so hard to give. You would agree then that in order to sustain a long-lasting, healthy, and burning love, you have to work hard at understanding your partner's main emotional communicator, or love language, as it is now popularly called.

How do you most like to show your love? Is that the same way your partner feels loved? In a more realistic sense, do you think your partner feels loved enough at this point in your relationship? If you feel you are putting in your heart and soul into showing how much you love your partner, but they don't seem to acknowledge this and question your love still, then maybe it is time for you to reevaluate what you have been doing and change up some things. Perhaps your partner is seeking something different from you – their preferred way of feeling loved.

It is not enough to simply talk about all the communication strategies you can employ like active listening, asking questions, and so on if you don't understand your partner's emotional language because then you can never really communicate love effectively.

So, let us go back to the basics and try to understand the different kinds of people there are and how they communicate and receive love.

♯1 Using Affirmative Words

The use of words is one way in which some people express love. I call them the verbal communicators because they want you to say it as you feel it. This set of people thrive on compliments and words of appreciation. This is their language and they are most likely to reciprocate love in the same manner.

If you discover that you or your partner fit this

description, then it is important to understand how to communicate emotional love this way in order to channel it towards building a love that lasts. Dr. Chapman calls it "the use of words of affirmation" [14, 23]. So, these are not just any kind of words, but words used to affirm the love you share for your partner. They should, therefore, be positive, uplifting words.

When you make statements like "Wow, you look so pretty in that dress", "Your hair is so beautiful", "Thank you for doing the laundry today", "It means a lot to me that you are helping out in the garden", "I really love that suit on you", "You smell so nice", you are making affirmative words and it would send a message of love to your verbal communicator partner. Imagine if this was you as well and words make you feel loved. If your partner showers these kinds of words on you regularly, wouldn't you be the happiest person ever? And guess what? Your relationship would bloom as well because you are feeling loved all the time.

Here are a few tips on how to make the best of using words of affirmation to express love to the verbal communicator:

- **Give compliments:**

  Get into the habit of giving great compliments that would get your partner beaming with love. Don't be tired of doing it. Find out the one thing that is great about them every day and say it to them because they want to hear it. Say things like "I love your make up", "You did such a great job on the garden today", "You have such beautiful eyes", and "I love these new shoes".

- **Give genuine appreciation:**

  We know you probably appreciate your partner, but you need to start saying it if your partner likes to hear it because it tells them of your love for them. How hard could it be to say things like "Thank you for making dinner tonight", "I really appreciate you coming out with me tonight", "I just want to thank you for all the little things that you do to keep our home tidy"? Surely compliments can't be that hard? And if it is, perhaps because you were never used to getting appreciation in the past, then you can slowly learn. Make a note to remind yourself to appreciate your partner for something they have done for you or for the relationship. If you really want to communicate love to them this way, then, slowly and steadily, you just might get the hang of it.

- **Be genuine and honest with your words:** When giving a compliment or appreciation or even encouragement, you should show your partner that you mean it. Do not just say it because you feel your partner wants a compliment anyway. If something is wrong with a dress they are wearing, you should, by all means, let them know politely instead of faking a compliment about the dress. Do not throw out appreciation just so they can let you be; instead, your words should come from a place of love and respect for your partner. Even though you might initially not see the big deal in saying things like compliments, if it means a lot to them, then it should to you as well. Remember, the motive is to show them you love them, and this is the primary way they understand it. So, say it as you meant it and watch your partner feel loved.

- **Avoid sarcasm:**

  Do not sneer at or taunt your partner with affirmative words. The purpose will be completely lost and in place of that, you could up end up causing hurt or anger. It also shows a great deal of disrespect and disregard, which shouldn't be the case in a loving relationship.

- **Avoid flattery:**

  Sometimes we tend to flatter our partners with compliments that we do not really mean with the aim of perhaps getting a favor from them because we know they love compliments and positive words. This shouldn't be the case and it could mean that we are taking advantage of them for our own selfish gains. If you do this, you defeat the aim of communicating love. Flattery would not communicate love because most likely, your partner already knows the compliment or appreciation is not genuine. The real reason for using genuine words of affirmation should be doing something for the happiness of the one you love and respect.

- **Give encouraging and uplifting words:**
For the one who thrives on affirmative words, encouraging and uplifting words would go a long way to help when they are down or under pressure. It could be that they need to hear those words from you to ignite the passion they need to go into the next level of a challenge. Be present to give them the encouraging words they desire as this makes a whole lot of a difference to them. It could be an area where they feel insecure or a potential that is yet to be untapped. Go ahead and say those uplifting words to them. Tell them, "I believe so much in your potential to start your own business", "I know that you can do this", "This might seem like a failure but I am confident that you can try again". Let your

words be the wings on which they fly! Encouraging words go a long way to tell your partner that you are empathic; it tells them that you can see the world from their own perspective. It makes your partner realize that what is important to them is also important to you. Ultimately, it shows that you care and you will be there for them all the way.

- **Give kind and compassionate words:**
Love cannot exist without some kindness and you can't claim to love someone yet continue to speak to him or her harshly or unkindly. It simply doesn't suffice. A lot of factors come into play in forging kind and compassionate words. Your body language, facial expression, and even your tone of voice can send the wrong message when you are trying to convey love through words of affirmation. For example, if you were rushing out of the house and your partner is asking how the meal they prepared for you was, then you decide to shout something like "You know the food was good, I wonder why you always ask", just before leaving,

that could really hurt your partner's feelings and there was definitely no message of love conveyed. It could have taken just an extra five seconds of your time to stop, look at your partner and say, "The food was great as always, thank you. I will see you later". See the difference? You might have just made their day. For someone who receives love through words, they tend to read a lot of meaning from the words you say, so watch it – let your words be kind. Imagine as well if you had to grumble about helping out with the laundry or washing the dishes, even though you are offering to do something for your partner, your tone of voice and attitude sends them the wrong message; therefore, use the right tone. Some people are used to shouting and it seems like that's their normal tone of voice. Your partner might interpret this wrongly when you are trying to communicate in his or her own emotional language. You should work at practicing lowering your tone even if you have to do so in front of a mirror or ask them to help you out. Let your words be pleasing to your partner's ears when communicating love to them. Let the words send the message you want them to carry – a message of love. So, watch that tone and watch your choice of words as well.

- **Be innovative with your words:**
Who says you have to stand before your partner to say affirmative words all the time? Once in a while, you can try out new things like writing them a poem. Compose a beautiful love letter and have it tucked away in the pocket of their jacket, leave sticky notes on the fridge to say how much you love them, give them compliments in the midst of their friends. The list is endless and so should your imagination.

#2 Giving Quality Time

There is another group of people that communicate love primarily by giving or receiving quality time. These people continuously seek the undivided attention of their partners and when they get it, it sends a message of love to them. You might ask yourself "But we live in the same house, what more does she/he want?" "We spend almost every evening together, what more does he/she want?" "I quit working weekends just to be with her, what more does she want?" These are questions we ask when we don't understand this method of communicating love. You feel you are available and can't understand why your partner still feels unloved and unhappy. You can hear complaints like "I feel like I am alone in this relationship" from your partner. What are they really trying to tell you? Do you feel like they are hard to please or over-demanding of you? If this seems like a common occurrence in your relationship, then your partner might just be one of the many people who receive love by quality time and maybe you have been doing this wrong. At the beginning of relationships, we want to be with our partners all the time. We want to hold hands, gaze into each other's eyes and talk without paying attention to all the interruptions. At that stage, there was a lot of quality time being shared by both of you and this kept your partner happy and full of love. You should ask yourself if you still spend that kind of time with your partner as much as you used to – time that is just for the both of you and not time spent watching TV or going over social media updates. You see, when you combine TV or something else with spending time with your partner, then your attention may be divided between that thing and them. This is not to say that you can not both watch TV, but if it was to convey a message of love, then the motive should be spending time with your partner to show love rather than the suspense that the movie carries. The quality time communicator wants your undivided attention when you chose to spend time with them and if you want to speak their love language, then you might have to start making some adjustments to your idea of "giving your time". It could be taking solo walks around the park or planning date nights just for the two of you once a week or taking a picnic together somewhere away from the world where you can just sit, talk, and laugh. To this kind of communicator, what matters really is the quality time you have just spent with them and that you are showing them that you love them.

Improving Quality Time Spent With Your Partner

If you determine to improve the quality time spent with your partner, then some of these facts to note about quality time may potentially help you out.

- **Quality time involves both parties being together:**

   Spending time together as a pair should be a goal if you seek to work on this emotional language. Being together does not necessarily refer to the proximity between both of you. You might live in the same house, sit on the same couch, and even sleep on the same bed, but still not spend quality time together. This love language requires attention rather than close proximity – focusing solely on each other for that period of time. You might be engaged in an indoor board game together or perhaps a game of tennis, but the primary reason is giving yourselves the attention and not the game. So, togetherness is more of an emotional connection you derive from giving each other undivided attention.

- **Quality time involves having quality conversations:**
  If and when we decide to set time aside to be with our partner, with the aim of spending quality time with them, then whatever conversations we have should be of quality too. The conversation should be warm, friendly, and uninterrupted. It should be a safe space where you can share your thoughts, feelings, and experiences without being judged. If your partner's language is quality time, then you might want to allow them to speak while you listen to what they have to say with keen and genuine interest. This tells them that you love them and are there for them to listen without judging. This is what gets them emotionally – not necessarily the talking, but the time and undivided attention you are giving to them. Perhaps your partner just wants to talk to you sometimes, not seeking your advice or opinion but just seeking your listening ear and your

genuine sympathy. It means you have to be a good listener too as listening involves giving attention. Dr. Chapman and a lot of other relationship experts suggest these tips for improving our listening experience when dealing with a partner whose primary love language is quality time [14, 16, 20].

o Try not to interrupt when your partner is speaking

o Try to maintain good eye contact with your partner as they talk

o Pay undivided attention and don't scroll on your phone or turn on the TV while they are still talking

o Ask for clarification if you don't understand the point they are making

o Be mentally present as much as possible. Don't go wondering about your favorite football club or what to make for dinner. If you do this, then you are not really listening, and the attention seeker might notice this even though you are looking them right in the eyes.

- **Quality time involves doing activities together:**

Imagine your partner loves to bake as a hobby and you probably don't like to. Then one day, you offer to bake with them, doing all the wrong things of course, but with a keen interest to learn. They seem happy and laugh at the silly mistakes you are making, but they are feeling loved. Even though you are not really helping and the baking and clean up would probably take longer than expected, you are spending time with them doing something that they love to do. The quality time seeker perceives this as a strong emotional connection. All they see is your expression of love to them and your undivided attention. So, as long as the motive is expressing love to each other, try doing things together that either both of you love to do or at least one person loves to do, and the other person doesn't really mind doing it as well. Whatever makes you spend quality time with your partner, from being together to talking to taking solo walks or playing games together, make a point of note to pay them your undivided attention and the message of love will be passed across soon.

♯3 Giving Gifts

The giving of gifts really cannot be separated from love and besides, who doesn't appreciate a well thought out gift once in a while? Gifts are a great way of expressing your feelings for your partner, but there are some to whom the receiving of gifts means more than to others. To this set of people, a gift from their partner is a symbol or expression of love towards them.

What really are gifts, and do they need to be bought and wrapped in fancy paper with a big bow tied across? The answer is - not exactly. Gifts really can be anything and do not have to always be expensive. As long as you have your partner in mind when planning, purchasing, or making the gift, then it is an expression of love. It could be a wild rose you picked on your way home or a hand-carved wooden love shape; a gift is what it is as long as it conveys your feelings to your partner.

While some people come from backgrounds where exchanging gifts is a part of their upbringing or culture, others were not as exposed to this practice, and this experience could affect their attitude towards giving gifts to their partners later on in life. They probably do not understand why their partner complains a lot about not getting them anything when it's not even their birthday and it might take a while to read the cues as this is not their primary emotional language.

Attitude To Money

This does not necessarily have to do with whether you have a surplus or are in lack; it's more of your mentality. Some people are natural spenders while others are savers or withholders. Those who are naturally very liberal with money may not have much of an issue giving gifts to their partners regularly because it comes naturally to them. On the other end, those who are natural savers would have to learn the act of giving gifts to their partners consciously, especially if this is the way they receive love primarily. Whether you are rich or poor, a giver of gifts would always find a way to give their partner something special once in a while.

Getting Into The Habit Of Giving Gifts

If you discover that receiving gifts is the primary way your partner feels loved and perhaps this is not your own language, then I guess you have to maximize this strategy in order to keep your partner feeling loved and maintain a thriving relationship. Here are some tips that can help you build up a habit of giving your partner gifts:

- **Remember, gifts don't have to be expensive:**
  There is no need to be running your pocket dry all the time because you want to please your partner

with a special gift. Get something that says, "You mean a lot to me and I love you". If your partner loves and understands you, then they'd probably understand your financial situation as well and wouldn't expect you to go above your means to please them.

- **Gifts don't have to be given only on special occasions:**
For those who grew up receiving gifts only on birthdays and Christmas, there is a need to greatly improve on that routine now. Give gifts to your partner on special days and beyond the birthdays, Valentine's days and Christmas. Give a random gift on a random day, when nothing is being celebrated. If your partner means that much to you, then they are worth celebrating every now and then. Remember, this communicates your affection to them, so start now. Pick something on your way back from work – a lovely card, a box of chocolates, a rose flower – give it to them and do it again soon – they will be filled with love. There

doesn't have to be a specific routine to it like every Friday or Sunday; bring in the element of surprise and get them something when they least expect it - you won't regret it.

- **Offer the gift of your presence:**
Gifts are not only physical items. It could be offering to escort your partner to a work event or planning a getaway trip as a surprise for your partner. Let them know you thought about the best gift to give to them on that occasion and you have chosen to offer your presence instead. Hopefully, they would be delighted.

Help! I Don't Know What Kind Of Gifts To Give My Partner

For someone who is not used to the habit of giving gifts, this might just be your cry for help. You are probably wondering how you are supposed to develop a lifestyle of giving gifts. What if you run out of ideas? Some people spend the better part of the year wondering what to get their partners for Christmas only to now realize that their partner wants much more because it is the fundamental way they feel loved. So how can you keep this practice going? Here are some tips that can help:

- **Keep a note of the things they love and update your list whenever you discover a new thing or a new idea.**
  This means you have to pay attention to the things they might admire in the shops, while watching TV, or while out with friends. It doesn't mean you have to get them whatever they admire – it just means you can get some inspiration about what they really like and what they don't. Also, listen to when they talk about something they wished they had that might make their life better or something you hear them say they are planning on getting.

  For example, if your partner keeps talking about how their shoes are all over the place and how they are planning to get a good shoe organizer, this could be a clue for a gift. If you are really attentive to your partner, then that list of yours will keep getting longer and longer and hopefully you won't run out of ideas soon.

- **Pay attention to the things in your surroundings:**
Perhaps when driving by an open market or a supermarket clearance sale, you could stop by and take a look. Who knows, there might be something there that calls out to you or something you are convinced your partner would like and who knows, it may be inexpensive too!

- **Ask family and friends:**
It is not wrong to seek some advice from either of your families or your partner's friends. For example, a lady's friends might just give you a great clue on a feminine gift you are planning to get, and a guy's friends might help you pick out a suit or a tie for your male partner.

- **Test the waters:**

  You can try out different gifts to see how your partner reacts to them, especially if you are just getting to know your partner's gift preferences. Buy a bunch of chocolate - see how they like it. Next time try out a new fragrance. You just might find out that they prefer fragrances to chocolate. Hopefully, in time, you would get a hang of the items they prefer. Don't forget to update your list on your notebook or electronic device. Remember, this takes off the pressure of having to decide all the time.

- **Ask the question:**

  There's absolutely nothing wrong with asking your partner for their gift preference once in a while, especially if you are going to buy something expensive and you know your partner to be quite specific with something like clothes. Some people like to choose what they want and that's not wrong – this is just so that they don't end up tossing the gift aside and hurting your feelings, so know when to ask.

♯4 Doing Acts Of Service

When you first fell in love, the need to do things for your partner most likely came to you naturally and you were consumed by trying to please them. They need not ask it sometimes. You may just find yourself offering to put their shoes away, hang their coats, organize their closet, do the dishes, make them dinner, and so on. A time comes when the "in love" phase wears out and you realize that you are faced with a partner who gradually stops doing things for you that you would have loved for them to do or perhaps they had done in the past. For the person who receives love from acts of service, this is the point where they start to doubt their partner's feelings for them. They begin to wonder what has gone wrong and if the love their partner had for them was suddenly evaporating. Your partner might most likely still love you but doesn't understand that this is your primary emotional language and so the complaints and arguments gradually set in. Again, a person's background can come into play in affecting the way they respond to performing acts of service for their partner. Suppose a guy was raised in a home where he was used to seeing his mother do all the household chores like cooking, cleaning, and laundry. He could grow up with this mentality and have a hard time later on in a relationship where his female partner keeps asking him to do domestic chores. It is most likely not the guy's primary language, so he finds it hard to adjust and on the other end, his "acts of service" communicator partner continues to feel unloved.

Acts of service are simply what it is called – extending gestures of service to your partner as a way of expressing your love for them. It includes any acts really, from small things like taking their coats and hanging it up to bigger things like repainting their bedrooms or building them a new wardrobe. As long as it is done from a place of love and the motive is to convey love to your partner, it is an act of service.

How To Improve On Your Acts Of Services To Your Partner

- **Ditch the stereotype:**

  If you want to express love to the "acts of service" communicator and you want to enjoy a happy and healthy relationship with them, then get ready to ditch the stereotype behavior that might have been formed by culture or upbringing, which probably limits men and women to certain acts and forbids that a man or woman should do this or that in a relationship. If you never experienced this issue, then other pointers might help.

- **Have an open mind towards service:**

  Consider the things you do for your partner as services of love; therefore, have an open mind to helping out or doing things that would make your partner feel loved and happy. It's a relationship between the both of you, so give it your absolute best. Do that odd favor for them and they would be pleased.

- **Do it happily:**

  Show your partner that you love them and that's why you are doing something for them. There is no point grumbling about while doing something for your partner or reminding them constantly that you are only doing them a favor. The message of love is not conveyed here, and that service is just a waste of an opportunity to show love. Instead, when you offer or accept to do a service for your partner like washing the dishes, offer to do it nicely and with a smile. Let them know it means a lot to you that you can do something for them.

- **Start with small things:**

  If you are new into conveying love this way and are not sure where to start, then start small. Offer to put the dishes away after a meal. Offer to get the post from the door or to make the bed. I bet when you see how your partner responds to these things, it will motivate you to do even more for them.

- **Learn how to do some things you didn't know how to:**

  Perhaps you wished you could help out with the cooking someday. You really want to help, but you have no idea how to even boil an egg! You can learn if you are serious about doing this act of service for your partner. Imagine you enroll at a weekend cooking course or start watching YouTube videos, then you eventually learn how to put together a nice breakfast. One morning, you are feeling not so confident, but you announce to your partner that you want to make breakfast, and then you actually pull it through. How do you think that would make them feel? So full of love, I'd guess. Now even though those eggs might be half-burnt or half-cooked, your partner feels loved because of what you just did for them, which they can see was out of love.

- **Ask them what they need:**

  If you are unsure what your partner needs help with, you can simply ask them. You can say: "What can I do to make your week less stressful?" "How can I help with dinner?" If you are a receiver of acts of service, then you should ask for your partner's help with love and respect and not nagging. Don't say statements like "Are you really watching TV while I slave out making you dinner?" "You know I need help, why do you always have to wait for me to ask?" Ask politely and with love and don't forget to appreciate your partner too when they do something for you – it could motivate them to do more, who knows!

- **Surprise them:**
Once in a while, surprise your partner who thrives on acts of service. Get home early and make dinner before they get back. Set the table beautifully and let them come home to meet a piping hot dinner already served, even though it was their turn to cook that evening.

♯5 Touching

Ever wondered why, when a friend is deeply saddened, you impulsively want to reach out and give them a hug or hold their hands or just give them a friendly pat at the back? What is it you are trying to demonstrate by hugging or holding hands? These gestures alone can bring a lot of comfort to the person involved. Whether you realize it or not, you are sending a message of love and comfort to your friend – to help share in their pain, and in turn, they receive your emotional connection and feel better.

Physical touch is such a strong communicator of love. Psychology has proven for a long time how much impact touching can have on an individual's life. It has shown that a child who was touched a lot by their parents (and other family members) by means of hugs, kisses, and cuddles turns out to be more emotionally stable than a child who was starved of physical touch [1, 6].

In love relationships as well, the power of physical touch cannot be overemphasized. Holding hands, hugging, kissing, foreplay and sexual intercourse, communicate the feeling of love to your partner. Even though sex is a very important aspect of touching, this method of communicating emotional love is not limited to sex alone.

Throughout the body, there are many touch receptors that carry signals to the brain to interpret. When touch happens, the brain can interpret these signals as different sensations including pain and pleasure [1]. This is why, to the one who communicates emotional love primarily through touch, it is so important what kind of signals you are giving to them. If you have discovered that touching is what makes your partner feel loved, then you have to learn to do it right.

Here are some pointers to help improve your experience of touching as a means of communicating love to your partner:

- **Remember that small gestures can go a long way:**

  When passing by your partner on the corridor, try rubbing your shoulder across theirs consciously and making some eye contact. It can send a deeper message of love than you think. Other conscious acts like rubbing their backs, giving a light massage, rubbing their feet, touching their face, or holding their hands are subtle but great ways you can improve on touching your partner.

- **Frequent hugs and kisses:**

  While this may be natural for some, others can find it hard to give hugs and kisses frequently. How many hugs are too much? It is like asking how much love is too much, so don't keep tabs. Learn to hug your partner that thrives on touch and loves to be touched. Give them a hug before you leave the house, when you get back, and when you get a random chance. Be liberal with your hugs and give kisses too – it can only make your partner feel loved and satisfied. Chances are they would reciprocate the love in your own love language so both of you are emotionally satisfied.

- **Give touching your full attention:**
Pay attention to your partner, especially during foreplay and sex. Do not be in a hurry to get into the sex act so you can get it over with. Give foreplay some time and attention. Look your partner in the eyes – let them know you desire to show them just how much they mean to you. Be patient – let your partner guide you to places where they feel pleasure the most and don't assume you know their body better than they do, even after years in the relationship. Explore new places to touch on their bodies and let them give you feedback. This will give you back a happy, loving, and satisfied partner, and a great sexual experience too.

- **Don't be afraid to touch your partner in public:**

When you are out on dates or just taking walks, reach out and hold their hands, touch their face, or touch their hair. When you are hanging out with friends or family as well, give the occasional touches – place your hand on theirs or let your feet touch theirs under the table. This shows that you are not afraid to show them love, even before their family or friends or neighbors. You are proud of the love you share, and you want them to keep that in mind.

Tips To Discovering The Primary Way You Or Your Partner Communicates Love

People might ask the question – how do I know what my primary emotional language is? "My partner loves gifts and also loves to get appreciated, how do I know which one is his primary language?" Now for some people, it is pretty straightforward, and you don't have to think too far before realizing what really speaks love to them, but for some others, you have to watch out for some cues to be certain. Here are some tips that can help:

- **Think of what you desire from your partner above everything else:**

  What is that thing that you really wished your partner would do above everything else? Would you rather they helped out with chores than buy you countless gifts or say how beautiful you are a million times? Would you rather have quality time with your partner? Then perhaps you have found your primary emotional love language. Think of your partner as well – what do they complain about wanting from you the most? A helping hand, attention, touch, or gifts?

- **Think of what your partner fails to do or what they say that hurts you the most:**

  This is another way to look at it. What is that one thing that your partner wouldn't do that brings hurt to you? Perhaps you wished you would get some more of their attention or they would just say 'thank you' for the things you do for them. This speaks to words of affirmation and the quality time seeker. Is this you or your spouse?

- **Think of what you have requested most from your partner:**

  Think of what you are always asking for. Do you frequently ask if you can spend time doing something together? Or ask if they can come home earlier for no special reason? Then you may be seeking quality time. How does it make you feel when your partner honors your request? If you feel loved, then you have just discovered your emotional language. Or are you always asking your partner how you look? Or do you ask your partner to say the words to you instead of keeping it in? You might thrive on words of affirmation.

- **Think of what you do to show love to your spouse:**

  Are you inclined to touching your spouse or buying gifts for them or perhaps just naturally helping them out? This might just be your own language too. It might also be a practice you have picked up from growing up, so think of the other cues as well to be sure about what really makes you feel loved.

Chapter 5: Safe And Secure Conversations - Getting Rid Of Judgments, Assumptions And Unhealthy Arguments

Communication in its entirety involves a whole lot of factors coming together. It goes beyond just sitting and having a conversation with your partner. Rather, communication is made up of factors that contribute to a healthy connection in a relationship. This means a combination of both verbal and physical skills in the right proportion.

All that said, we still cannot underplay the role of great verbal communication in relationships. Talking to each other is such a powerful tool that keeps relationships running smoothly, and the day a couple stops talking is the day their relationship begins to have frictions.

So how can we develop and maintain a healthy, 'talking' relationship – one in which we are able to effectively communicate our needs to our partners with the confidence that we are being heard? How can we continuously converse with each other without the fear of being misinterpreted or judged? Can we really sustain a decent conversation that is void of unnecessary arguments?

In a love relationship involving two adults, there just might be nothing worse than not being able to freely speak your mind with your partner. A lot of people find that they gradually begin to bottle up their real feelings and opinions just to avoid an argument or wrong judgment from their partner. This should not be the case in a healthy relationship. It becomes injurious when a partner continues to withhold feelings that should be talked about and, with time, the lack of expression can lead to huge misunderstandings, low self-esteem, bitterness, and even hatred.

In this chapter, we will discuss communication patterns and strategies that can build up and maintain healthy and secure conversations within couples in every instance.

Voice Tone: Pitch, Pace, Volume, And Timbre

Your voice tone is such an important aspect of communicating with your partner clearly. The way you use your tone can speak a lot more than the actual words that you are saying, so there is a need to get this important skill right. Imagine if you had to say the words "I am sorry" to your spouse and you say it with such a sarcastic tone; the message that those words contain is not conveyed; instead, your partner might actually find your communication to be offensive, demeaning, insulting, and hurtful. Imagine as well that you say the same words in such a hushed manner or with a shout. What message are you communicating then to partner? - Certainly not the genuine apology that those beautiful words are meant to convey. This tells us how powerful the tone of a person's voice can affect what they are actually saying. Researchers from the University of Southern California have explained just how critical a person's tone of voice can affect the success of their relationship. In a 2015 research study where they looked at a whole lot of couples' voices for a period of time, they discovered that the success or failure of a couple's relationship can be better predicted by their voices rather than their behavior [27]. Therefore, we can affirm that communication borders a lot on how you say something as well as what you are actually saying. We will consider four important aspects of the voice tone: pitch, volume, pace, and timbre [15].

- **Pitch:**
  This is simply the degree of highness or lowness of your voice as it fluctuates at any given time. When you are speaking to your partner and you are using a very high pitch, it can suggest that you are trying to be defensive or simply immature. A higher pitch can also appear to be less affirmative in a sentence and can sometimes sound like a question, which can cause confusion. A pitch that is too low can also make you appear unserious and less affirmative, so

you need to find the right balance for your tone at every time. This means you have to be conscious of your pitch and learn to adjust appropriately if you notice you are going too high or even too low.

- **Pace:**

  This is simply how fast or how slow you are speaking. We find that some people tend to speak really fast in the middle of an argument, perhaps because they are agitated or just want to get everything out before their partner cuts in. There is a need to get mindful of your voice pace in addition to your voice pitch when having conversations with your partner. Talking calmly and slowly gives your partner a better chance to catch and absorb everything that you are saying as opposed to talking too fast, which can make them lose focus and miss out on important details of your speech. It becomes harder to listen and follow attentively when you are going too fast, so become aware of your pace and slow down if you notice you are going too fast. One trick is to pay attention to your partner's facial expression to see if they are losing concentration. That can help you to pause and adjust your pace to a more regular rhythm. Be mindful not to talk too slow as well as it can appear disrespectful and offensive. The right approach to your voice pace should be speaking evenly and steadily.

- **Volume:**

This is how loud you are speaking. Volume can become a common problem with arguments, as a lot of people tend to raise their voices or yell when they are angry. Shouting at your partner is such a dangerous tool in conversations. There is nothing positive that can come from shouting at your partner. Rather, you won't get listened to and your message will not be passed across. Yelling will most likely stir your partner to do the same as well, which can lead to a ripple effect of anger, malice, and hurtful words. The emotional damage that yelling can cause can really be avoided if we start to pay attention to the volume of our tone. You don't need to shout to emphasize a point; you can rather try slowing the pace of your voice and gently highlight the point that you are trying to make, giving your partner time to take it in. Remember that yelling most likely leads nowhere, so get in control of your volume. If you notice you are getting really angry, then try this technique – pause the conversation for a while. Let your partner know that you would like to have some time to cool off before continuing the conversation. Do something that can really calm you down like playing a game or watching a comedy show. When you feel much better, invite your partner to continue the conversation where you know you can now be in control of your tone (especially your volume).

- **Timbre:**
This speaks of the emotional aspect of your voice. What kind of attitude do you put up as you speak to your partner? Remember that your partner can perceive your attitude, and this can affect their understanding of what you are saying. So, the next time you are having a conversation with your

partner, take note of how you really sound. Do you sound happy, sad, in a hurry, sarcastic, or simply frustrated? These are emotions that can easily be perceived in your tone. Become aware of your emotions as you speak and try to manage them appropriately so your partner doesn't misinterpret your message.

The Use Of Words: Non-Judgmental Communication

Judgments are usually made from our own personal opinions of things and how they should be without exactly accessing the facts and reality before us. A judgmental mindset can hugely impair the way we understand our partner during conversations and communication in general. It also affects our clarity to reason as, most likely before we can properly consider the facts, we have already formed an opinion in our minds [21].

A lot of wrongful criticism and accusation spring from

a judgmental mindset; the result of which can be very detrimental to effective and healthy communication in relationships. Many people are even unaware that they judge their partners through their language and attitudes during communication; hence, we will look at pointers, which can help you examine your communication for judgmental language or behavior.

What Judgment Really Tells Your Partner

When you are quick to judge, it tells your partner that:

- You are jumping into conclusions all by yourself
- You are not really listening to what they are saying
- You are not looking at things from their own perspective
- You are selfish
- They can't be open-minded with you all the time
- You are not paying attention to their feelings
- They can't feel safe and secure while talking to you
- You can't be trusted completely

I believe it is important to realize the existence of a problem before looking for a solution to it. So, think about the last conversation you had with your partner that probably didn't go quite so well. Do you think that perhaps there was some element of judgment in your conversation? If you are unsure, consider some of these pointers.

1. **Do you listen to your partner all the way before coming to a conclusion?**

   Listening all the way is very important so you can weigh in everything that your partner is saying. Listen to understand and not just so you can respond. Most times, when you interrupt your partner, it means that you already have an opinion in your mind without considering everything they have to say; after all, you didn't hear them out completely. Most likely, you may have missed out on some of the details of their message. So, the next time you are tempted to cut in too soon with your opinion, beware that this might just be a red flag for passing judgment.

2. Do you forge your opinion based on what you know about your partner or their actual claim during a conversation/argument?

Imagine your partner fails to get some agreed-upon grocery items from the store and you realize this in the evening when you both get back and these are very necessarily household items. You are probably getting upset.\

Perhaps they had made similar errors in the past and that comes to your mind immediately and the following conversation ensues:

You: "Did you pick up the items we need from the store?"

Your partner: "I'm sorry I couldn't get them. I was stuck in ...."

You: "It's ok, I know, you forgot again"

Your partner: (feels hurt by your conclusion. He was going to say the store was closed by the time he got there due to closing work late and getting stuck in heavy traffic)

The example above is typical of making conclusions based on what you know of your partner, probably capitalizing on their weaknesses instead of giving them the chance to bring in new details. This is judgmental and can cause hurt and misunderstanding in a relationship.

3. **Do you usually ask the reason why your partner said or did something so as to gain a better insight on the issue at hand?**

Instead of making wrongful assumptions, the best thing to do when you are unsure of your partner's opinion or actions is to ask them why. This is better than reaching conclusions on your own because then you are most likely to be influenced by your own opinion and reasoning. So, even if you have known your partner for fifty years, there is no guarantee that you can always be 100% right about them. The practice of asking why will give you a better insight into what your partner's mindset is on an issue and it will give them the opportunity to explain themselves too.

4. Do you ask for your partner's opinion on a matter before reaching a conclusion?

When you are in the habit of assuming that you know what your partner's opinion will be on a matter, then you are treading on judgmental grounds. Give your partner the opportunity to speak their own opinion on a matter even if you think you know them too well. What if you assume wrongly someday and hurt your partner? Besides it shows how much you value their opinion and that you respect them enough to hear their thoughts on a matter. So quit being the judge, just ask them.

5. Do you keep facts focused on the current situation or continue to refer to the past?

Referring to your partner's past life and mistakes in a current situation means you are being judgmental. When you have chosen a life with someone you love and respect, then their past shouldn't matter to you anymore and by no means should you judge them by their past mistakes. Instead, focus solely on the current situation and the facts before you. Ask questions and try to understand their current position before giving your own opinion.

Language: Right Or Wrong?

Language is also a very important factor in creating and maintaining judgment-free conversations; words, they say, are very powerful [21]. They have been known to make or mar great relationships. This is why it is so important to use the right words to convey your message all the time – words that say you care about your partner enough to listen to what they are saying and not to judge or reach conclusions easily. There is a right and wrong way to pass on an opinion. There are words that I strongly advise that you avoid because they can immediately be interpreted as judgmental. Here are a couple of examples:

Instead of saying...	I should say...
That's wrong	I have a different opinion/view of this
The fact is	Here's what I understand
This is how it is	This is how I see it
This is unreasonable	I don't really get how this works out/how exactly will it work?
It doesn't make sense	I don't understand/ I don't follow
You are doing it all wrong	This looks different from what I expected
That's a lie	I am confused about this
This has nothing to do with X	I don't get how this relates to X
That's unfair	Can we find what is fair for both of us
You make me feel	I feel
What wrong with you?	Is there something you think I should know?
How could you be so	I would love if you explained to me why you
I cant believe you did X	What really happened?
You haven't done X	How about this task? Where are we with completing it?

Some General Advice On Achieving Safe And Judgment Free Conversations

- **Pay attention to non-verbal communication:**

  When listening to your partner, you should pay attention as well to non-verbal cues like eye contact and body language. Are they feeling afraid, anxious, or happy? Are they relaxed? Do they appear uncomfortable? All these should speak to you as well as what they are saying, so pay attention so you can understand them clearly. On your own part, you should maintain eye contact and nod your head to encourage where necessary.

- **Show regard for your partner:**
Don't assume you know what they want to talk about. Allow them to express themselves while you listen. Don't interrupt while they speak. Take the talk seriously and don't make funny remarks on what they are saying. Let your partner know that you respect them and whatever their concern is will be taken seriously by you.

- **Don't be manipulative:**
Don't introduce sex or distractions when your partner really wants to talk about something serious. Postponing the issue will not take it away.

- **You don't have to always be right:**

Learn to make compromises and meet your partner somewhere in the middle. You don't always have to have the last say. It is not a competition.

Chapter 6: Active Listening

"You are not listening to me" "Did you hear what I just said?" "Are you here? Aren't you going to say something?" These sentences may sound familiar as they are examples of popular complaints we give or get when it seems like our partner is not really listening to what we are saying, even though they are right there in front of us. Everyone likes to be listened to and no one likes to be ignored or taken for granted while they are speaking.

But how can we become effective listeners who listen with rapt attention, being totally present and not just with the aim of waiting to give a response? We must realize that listening is the most important aspect of interpersonal relationships. A more tactical way to listen, called 'active listening', can solve the listening issues that a lot of relationships experience. It involves actively listening to a speaker, employing the use of all our senses in the listening act [34].

It not only involves giving your full attention to the speaker but must also convey a conviction to them as well that they are being listened to or else they might start to feel like they are being ignored.

Active listening involves the use of both verbal and nonverbal cues by the listener, which conveys the right message of listening to the speaker. Non-verbal signals involve actions like head nods, eye contact, body language, posture, and smiles. Verbal signals refer to saying things like 'yes' or "mmhmm" as you listen. The combination of some or all of these signals convinces the speaker that you are listening and encourages them to keep talking with the ease that they seek.

Characteristics Of An Active Listener

- **They make eye contact:**
  Have you ever experienced a situation whereby you had to talk to someone and, while you spoke, they wouldn't even look at you? How did that make you

feel? Like they were ignoring you, I'd guess. That's how important eye contact is. It is a very important way to show the speaker that they have your attention and you are focused on what they are saying. Of course, eye contact can be intimidating for some shy people, especially when speaking to someone really superior to you, but it is definitely a good practice that we can master in dealing with people in general.

- **They assume the right posture:**
Let us look at, for instance, the difference between leaning forward and leaning backward on a couch while listening to someone in a very serious conversation. Leaning forward, added with good eye contact, will probably convince the speaker that you are listening attentively to them as opposed to leaning backward, which depicts more reduced attention.

- **They give smiles:**

Smiling occasionally is a way of showing attention, agreement, or showing that you are happy with what the speaker is saying. It can further convince the speaker that, not only are you are paying full attention to them, but you also understand what they are saying. So, small smiles once in a while are a great advantage for an active listener.

- **They avoid distractions:**
An active listener is expected to be giving their full attention. Doing things like looking at your wristwatch or the clock while listening can distract you and your speaker. Other activities like picking nails, fidgeting, or playing with an object while listening can also be distracting.

- **They can reflect the speaker's facial expression:**
Active listening also involves mirroring the speaker's facial expression to show emotions like empathy or sympathy, depending on the situation. For example, if a friend is telling you the story of

how they lost a loved one in a car crash and you are actively listening, they are probably putting up a sad face and you should too. If you just sit there, nodding your head with such a straight face, chances are you are not really listening to what they are saying. Try not to mimic the speaker though. There is a big difference between reflecting and mimicking facial expressions. Mimicking can send off the wrong message – it shows that you are not really listening for sure and it can be insulting to the speaker.

- **They ask relevant questions:**
  Asking questions can show the speaker that you are following what they are saying. You need to ask questions that are directly related to what the speaker is saying though.

Don't go asking why they have a redeye when they are talking about expanding their business with you. It shows you are not listening to what they are saying, so keep the questions relevant to the discussion. You can ask about the eye later. Questions help the speaker to clarify what they are saying so you can better understand them. Ask at the right time – when you get a chance to speak. Do not interrupt the speaker while they are still speaking in order to ask your question.

- **They are capable of repeating or paraphrasing what the speaker has just said:**
When you paraphrase what the speaker is saying once in a while, it shows your comprehension of the message and encourages your speaker to continue.

- **They are capable of remembering:**
Your ability to remember what the speaker was talking about, even after the conversation is over, shows you were actively listening. If after some time, you find that you can't really remember the highlights of what the speaker was saying, then it means you were not really giving your full attention to your speaker.

- **They are capable of summarizing what the speaker has said:**
  When your speaker is done talking, it is a great thing to repeat the key points of what the speaker has just said to show that you got the whole gist and understood their message. It again affords the speaker the opportunity to clarify any misunderstood points.

Active Listening In Romantic Relationships

Relationships involve a whole lot of communication to keep afloat. Therefore, active listening is such an important tool for both parties involved in the relationship. Active listening is very important in relationships to encourage your partner's openness, which in turn reduces the chances of misunderstandings. This method of listening will also help in resolving conflicts more easily and it can build or enhance trust amongst partners.

In relationships, what a lot of people do is listening to respond and not listening to understand. Those who decide to and become committed to listening to understand will eventually promote a more satisfying experience in their relationships than others [16].

- **It takes practice:**
  There is quite a considerable amount of mental and emotional energy that goes into active listening, so it takes time to master. At first, it might seem like you cannot maintain your concentration without wanting to respond or judge [5]. You keep fighting the urge to form your own opinion in your head and that affects your concentration too. Try to constantly remind yourself of your resolve to actively listen to your partner and consciously maintain that concentration. Be in control and in time, you will grow to get the hang of how it works.

- **Actively listening to your partner shows how much you care:**

Using active listening while your partner is speaking shows them that you have a great deal of care and respect for them and what they are saying. You care enough to listen to them with all your heart and mind because of how much they mean to you.

- **Active listening provides a safe space for your partner:**
  When your partner knows that they can talk to you and you can actively listen in a conversation without judging them, then they can feel safe and secure with you all the time. It gives your partner the opportunity to be open with you – to communicate the deepest part of their hearts and their fears too, knowing that their partner loves them enough to listen deeply.

- **It can help couples talk through the most difficult and uncomfortable conversations confidently:**

While active listening doesn't mean that you can breeze through a conversation with the right words to say, it gives you the gracefulness to talk through difficulty knowing that you are not going to suddenly be shouted at or attacked verbally, but that your partner is one who would patiently let you talk in an empathic atmosphere [5].

- **It deepens the bond between partners in a relationship:**
  When you have two active listeners in a relationship, it means that communication will be so much easier, and conflicts resolved faster. Both parties are comfortable talking with each other about anything without fear, creating room for closeness and intimacy.

- **It promotes intimacy:**
  When you are not afraid to talk to your partner about your sexual needs because you trust that they can listen to you without judging but seeking to understand you, then this technique can come in

handy to really improve a couple's sexual experience.

- **Do not give in to the temptation to interrupt your partner speaking:**
  Active listening requires that you do not interrupt your partner while they are still speaking. Remember that the reason for listening is to understand them and not so you can respond like so many people do. Sometimes, your partner might still be talking but take small pauses before continuing. This is not the time to cut in. Wait until you can see that they are finished or ask for your response. Ask them if you are unsure.

- **Remember that summarizing is a good trick:**
  When you summarize what your partner just said, highlighting the key points, it assures your partner that you indeed listened to everything they said. It also gives them a chance to clarify or elaborate on any misunderstood points. So, when you have just

summarized, you can add something like "Is that what you meant?" or "I hope I got you right." and wait for their acknowledgment before you continue talking.

- **Active listening is contagious:**
  Do not get disappointed if you feel your partner does not actively listen to you in conversations even though you practice active listening with them all the time. Don't worry – keep doing what you are doing whilst encouraging them to do so as well and soon you might realize they will start to copy your listening style as well. When your partner realizes how serious you take listening to them, it's only natural that they would start to follow suit, so be patient.

How To Resolve Conflicts In Relationships With Active Listening

When there is an unresolved conflict in a relationship, it is likely that the atmosphere is tense and there might be a bit of anger brewing up. How do you apply active listening to resolve a conflict whilst containing it and not allowing the situation to escalate into a big argument? Here are a few steps you can follow to help resolve things more easily.

- **Find the right time:**
  You know your partner and the best time to get them talking. Make sure to wait for the best time. For instance, there is no need to bring up a serious conflict when you know your partner has come in very late and is obviously tired. When they are tucked in bed and ready to sleep might also be a bad time. Find a time when they are in the best mood and would most likely actively listen to you as well.

- **Find the right words and then raise the issue:**
  Think of the right words to introduce the issue. Play it out in your mind before saying it, especially if the issue is a sensitive one. Be warm and polite with them. No need saying, "You know we have to talk

about this issue." Instead, you can say, "Is it ok for us to talk about this issue now?" When you start out the conversation right, chances are it might gradually proceed in the right direction.

- **Listen to their perspective:**
  It is now time to allow your partner to speak and for you to practice your active listening skills. Remember to concentrate as much as possible.

- **Ask appropriate questions if necessary:**
  Ask questions to better understand what they are saying, but don't interrupt them.

- **Summarize what you have heard:**
  When they have said their own perspective, summarize for them what you have just heard. You can start by saying, "So what you have just said is …"

- **Empathize with them:**

When you have summarized and are sure you understood all they have said, say something to empathize with them like, "I am really sorry you had to go through that", "I really understand that your job is very demanding", or "I can imagine how hard it must be for you".

- **Now it's your chance to talk:**
  Your active listening and empathy should have calmed down any anger brewing from your partner at least enough for you to start speaking. Go on and give your own perspective. Chances are your partner would listen to you now with the same attention you gave them. If they interrupt you, this does not have to lead to an argument. Apply your active listening skills again and then let them know that you wish they would listen to you just the way you have listened to them. Keep at it and don't blow it up.

The Active Listener's Creed

- I am an active listener
- I will deeply listen to my partner with the aim to understand them and not just to respond.
- I will focus on my partner and not myself as I listen
- I will not interrupt while they speak
- I will refrain from judging; instead, I will show empathy and sympathy always
- I will ask questions when I get the chance
- I will give my partner my full attention by maintaining eye contact and smiling occasionally to reassure them
- I will pay attention to their body language
- I will avoid any form of distractions while my partner speaks
- I will actively listen because I love my partner
- I will actively listen because I genuinely care

Chapter 7: Coping With Typical, Solvable Problems

As we have mentioned before, relationships take hard work. Even the most committed and loving relationships will face problems once in a while. Conflict resolution is always a challenge in many relationships and couples have different approaches to resolving their conflicts. They can arise from common issues like housework, stress, or finances. Conflicts can also come from having a new baby, sex, or even the in-laws [20].

These are areas where a lot of couples struggle with resolving conflicts and, if left unresolved, can really affect the stamina of a loving relationship or marriage. Most of the issues mentioned are solvable, meaning they are issues that can be successfully resolved if the right strategy is put in place and without causing major damages to the relationship. We see some of these issues on the rise in the last recent couple of decades as the world continues to advance. For instance, couples work more hours these years and are becoming more and more stressed as compared to the olden days where the man was seen as the provider for the home and the woman would stay at home as the home keeper, doing most domestic chores and looking after the children. The truth is, things have now changed and so have the challenges that relationships face. Not too long ago, you didn't have to bother that your partner was constantly attached to their phones or social media sites while you sought their attention on the dinner table because we didn't have those distractions at the time. We didn't have to worry about video games and smart devices. Some of these modern gadgets are beginning to take up much of the quality time we should be spending with our partners and families [18]. This is also causing a massive decrease in face-to-face communication [17] and it is affecting the way we are supposed to nurture a healthy and thriving relationship.

In this chapter, we will look at some common solvable problems faced by the twenty-first-century couple and suggest practical strategies with which they can be successfully resolved while keeping the relationship intact.

Electronic Distractions

While we place so much emphasis on quality communication between couples, especially face-to-face conversations, research has shown that with the invention of smart devices like phones and tablets, the actual time that couples spend talking to each other continues to decline [17, 18]. One research carried out in Los Angeles showed that the average time partners spent in face-to-face conversations were a mere thirty-five minutes a week [17]. This is not good, and you can imagine it will continue to get worse if strategies are not put in place to curb some of these distractions. You notice that even when a couple is out on a date, it can still be difficult for them to put aside their mobile phones and just focus on each other for that short period of time. This can really affect communication and quality time spent together. When a couple cannot communicate effectively, the long-term effect can be catastrophic as they gradually begin to drift apart without even knowing it and suddenly, two once-loving individuals become nothing short of total strangers to themselves, even though they may still be living in the same house. Couples need to assess how much time they spend on things like social media as opposed to how much time they spend giving to their relationship. If the time you spend chatting or going through social media sites on your device is more than the time you put into spending quality time with your partner or family, then you would agree that this is a red flag and the scales have to be tipped the other way round. So how can we solve this common solvable problem? Here are some practical tips that can help:

- **Accept that this is an issue that needs to be tackled:**
  If your partner is constantly complaining about how much time you are on your phone or glued to the TV as opposed to how much time you spend with them, then perhaps this is true. There's no

point trying to justify your actions or looking for whom to blame for this problem. Accepting one's fault shows great maturity in relationships, so if you are guilty, accept that you are. Don't say "You are always tired; that's why I am on my phone" or "You are never done in the kitchen; that's why I watch TV all the time". Making excuses will not help the matter, but could result in an unnecessary argument. Remember that your partner is bringing up the issue because they want more of your attention, which they feel starved of. If both of you are guilty of this distraction, then someone has to take the first step to initiate change before you grow further apart. Discuss this with your partner and come to an agreement that some changes have to be put in place. Sit down and agree on limits. Reaching an agreement on limitations to using your phone for texting and chatting shouldn't be so difficult, but you need to talk about it and arrive at an arrangement that is fair for both of you. Remember that your relationship is far more important than those people on social media sites or chat groups, whom you might never actually have a real relationship with so set your priorities right. For example, you can agree to put away your phones at mealtimes, when out on dates, and when you are having a serious discussion. Do whatever works for both of you as long as you are both happy with the arrangement.

- **Stick to the agreement:**
Show that you value and respect your partner and your relationship by honoring the agreement to put away phones and turn off the TV at certain times. At first, it might seem hard, but remember that these gadgets were not even in existence a few years ago and life went on quite alright, so you too can do without them for a couple of minutes or so. Instead, channel the time towards talking to your partner, building your relationship, and spending quality time with your family. If you have an emergency phone call, let your partner know how important the call is and that you have to take it. It shows how much regard you have for them.

Dealing With Stress

Stress can originate in relationships from a lot of factors, but most especially from work. A large percentage of couples in this modern age either work employed in an establishment, running their own business, or are self-employed. Each job comes with its own form of stress. Partner A is plagued with an over-demanding boss and a voluminous task to complete before the end of day and partner B is struggling to meet up with a customer's order deadline in their small packaging business. Both have had it to their necks for the day and return home to each other. Suddenly, something as small as a question turns into a heated argument. Both parties cannot understand why they are so irritated at each other. The truth is, they had let the stress take the better part of them and, even though it actually originated from work, it has now been brought into the relationship and home. This is a common feature in many relationships. Stress can lead to major conflicts if not managed properly and, since we really can't exactly prevent the stress in the first place, there is a need to learn how to better cope or handle it so it doesn't encroach into and affect our loving relationships. Here are some practical approaches that can help:

- **Find a way to unwind or distress after work:** At the end of a working day, acknowledge that you are stressed out and this means that you may need a few minutes to yourself to destress or "decompress" as Dr. Gottman of the book 'Seven Principles For Making Marriage Work' put it [20]. Find out a routine that can work effectively for you. Some people find taking a run immediately after work or going to the gym to be really relaxing and a great way to de-stress the whole work tension. They thereafter feel more relaxed to interact with their partner. Others find activities like taking a shower, meditating, or simply lying on the bed for a few minutes to really work for them. The point is to do something that soothes and relaxes the tension in your head. Your partner can also be a great way to de-stress with. A warm, soothing embrace can go a long way to calm you down, especially with the added emotional connection. A short session of shoulder massage from your partner can work too if it's, of course, convenient for them at the time. Once your de-stress activity is done, you can now go on to your routine at home and hopefully not nag about a simple question.

- **Remember it's the stress talking, not them:** If your partner comes home in a bad mood and suddenly snaps at the first thing you say, the tendency is for you to get upset, but this can lead to a totally unnecessary heated argument. You know your partner, they are not normally like that, so when you get that strange response or no response at all to the "How was your day?" question you just asked them, tell yourself it is the stress talking and not them. They would come around eventually.

- **Help your partner deal with their stress:**

Communication comes into play here as well. Talk to your partner about managing their stress if it is affecting you or the family. Ask them how you can help them deal with their stress after work or how both of you can help each other deal with your work-related stress so it doesn't affect your time together. Let them say how they feel and what might make the day feel better. Bring up any suggestions you have as well and hopefully, you can agree on a routine that works for both of you.

- **Be sensitive to your partner's feelings:**
  When your partner comes home from work looking all stressed out, that might not be the best time to bring up an unpaid bill or your son's upcoming PTA meeting. You know that a serious discussion at that time might not get you the answers you need, so why not give them a few minutes to destress and come back to you in a much better mood? You are likely then to have a more reasonable, conflict-free discussion, which is what we all want.

Money Matters

Money remains one of the biggest causes of conflicts in relationships and marriages [20]. Should you have a joint account? You want this but I want that instead. How do we reach an agreement on what to buy? Should your partner be spending that much on a car? How do you save up for this and that? Who pays which bill? Your partner earns more, shouldn't they contribute more to home expenses? Why do you have to be completely open to your partner on how you spend your money? The list is endless and so is the number of conflicts that money can cause, especially between two working adults. Many people don't want to talk about money before entering into relationships. You don't want to sound selfish or give your partner the impression that you are not a spender. But this here is a serious mistake since everyone has a different mentality of how to spend their money and what money means to them.

- **So, the first step to avoiding money conflicts is to talk about it in time.**

Ask your partner to tell you what money really means to them because money can signify a means of power to some and a source of security to others. It could also mean pleasure to some people, so talk about it. Does money make you feel secure, in charge, or just pleased? This can help when there is a money conflict – you can understand and tackle the underlying issue instead of just the person.

- **Budgeting is the next important tip to take note of.**

  This means sitting down to work out how you want to spend your money. You will need to outline your needs and wants. Include home needs like utility bills, mortgage, insurance, food, and upkeep for the kids, recreation, holidays, charity, and savings. Calculate how much these things will cost, bearing in mind the non-essential items like recreation, holidays, and charity [32]. You should agree on how much to spend on these kinds of items, and then calculate what your total expenses might seem like. Each person should state what he or she is comfortable contributing to the budget, bearing in mind individual earnings. It is now time to allocate the funds to the items on the list, adjusting where necessary to suit the budget. You should make sure that both of you are happy enough with your contributions and no one feels like the other is cheating them. You can make the budget at the beginning of the year and review it once in a while or as things change. You need to also decide how to manage the cash flow [32]. Some couples divide up the responsibilities; for example, one person pays the utility bills while the other pays for groceries. Some others just contribute the money monthly to a joint account and one person is agreed upon to manage the joint expenses and give an account to the other. The partner responsible is like the house manager. Taking care of bills and making sure payments are up to date and house needs are met. Whichever way you decide to go about it as a couple, as long as there is some serious planning ahead of time, budgeting and planning should take care of most of the money conflicts that can arise. There are so many resources out there on budgeting and money management. It could be a great investment to read some of them as this can give couples a wider range of strategies that can work with budgeting and financial planning.

- **Don't forget to discuss your separate needs as well:**
Talk about personal money plans as well. Is there something significant that you want to buy for yourself this year and you feel your partner should know about? Then you should let them know in time. It is great when both parties understand why some personal expenses are made even though "it is not your money". This can make your partner feel secure in the fact that you are not just going to wake up one morning and use up all your savings for some adventurous feat. Telling them also means they can chip in their own advice on what you chose to do with the money. Your partner feels carried along and important too.

- **Bear in mind the future:**

  Discuss your short and long-term goals with your partner – do you want to buy a house in the near future or perhaps start up a family business? How do you intend to save up for this? Maybe you want to start saving up for your retirement or your child's college. You need to agree on a plan that can help both of you reach your financial goals. The point to remember here is the need to work together and arrive at a decision that is accepted by both of you. There might be some sacrifice involved here and there. As long as you are happy to give up this or that so you can achieve something else, it's a win for both parties.

Dealing With The In-Laws

In-law issues are another source of conflict that couples face in marriages. It can bring in a lot of tension when your parents want to be involved in your lives and your partner thinks they are crossing their boundaries. These issues can arise at any point in a marriage and as changes occur, like when the children are born, when major milestones are achieved, and when parents get really old and are in need of care. A very common in-law rivalry is that between wife and mother-in-law. This happens because the wife wants her husband's full care and attention and her husband's mother can start to feel like she has suddenly been replaced and her son no longer loves her the way he used to. A husband can find himself caught in between this kind of rivalry and it can cause conflict between him and his partner. Here is some practical advice on how to deal with in-laws:

- **Communicate:**
  Psychologist Teri Apter says to maintain good communication with your parents and in-laws [4]. Talk to them about your boundaries and why it is important to you that they respect them.

- **Respect:**
  Try as much as possible to show a good level of respect and regard for your partner's parents, no

matter how difficult they might seem. Your partner should, in turn, show respect to your own parents too. Do not ridicule or dismiss them if a conflict arises. Show sympathy and be diplomatic. Focus on resolving the conflict rather than defaming the in-law involved. Remember that you just might become an in-law one day to someone else. So always treat them with kindness and respect.

- **Say to yourself "My partner comes first always":**

Your wife should come first before your mother and your husband should come first before your mother or father. This might not sound like the nicest thing to say but your marriage should be that important to you, so you should place your spouse first and before anyone else. Let your parents know so they can learn to respect this. They might not find it funny at first, but in time they will come to accept the changes. This is not to say that you should disregard or disrespect them by any means. You love your parents too, but you are building a life and family now with this special human who wants to feel respected and secure even in the eyes of your parents, so learn to stand up for your partner and take sides with them if it comes to that point.

- **Incorporate parents into family rituals once in a while:**
  You can choose one holiday to spend with your parents or invite them for a milestone celebration. If they live in the same vicinity with you, you can go on family dates with them once in a while just to show them that you value them enough to share some of your family experiences with them. This can help them feel content enough and respect your boundaries and family values. Be sure to discuss this with your partner and make sure they are comfortable with any arrangements before inviting any of the in-laws.

Dealing With Housework Conflicts

It is surprising how much conflict housework can

bring to a relationship. But when you have a partner that refuses to do his or her own share of the agreed tasks in the home, this can put a lot of pressure on the other person as well as offset the balance and structure of the house and relationship. Generally, women are probably more concerned about getting house chores done and keeping the home organized than men are. Some men can't understand why women make such a fuss about things like separating dirty laundry by colors or loading up the dishwasher before going to bed. Isn't it all dirty laundry that can be sorted out just before washing? Or can't we just load the dishwasher in the morning? Conflicts arise as well when women begin to feel like they are being overwhelmed with chores while the man is out at a game or watching TV. Wives tend to be more domesticated and this is simply because of the old-time tradition that labeled the woman as the home keeper and the man as the provider. But since the scales have tipped these days, and both men and women work, a woman can begin to feel disrespected, used, or unsupported when she doesn't get enough help from her partner. Again, here are some practical tips that can help resolve these kinds of issues:

- **Men should learn to do more housework to support their women:**

  You can get a lot from a woman when she sees you are helping out more with chores at home. A woman is more emotional and can be easily moved by her partner doing chores at home. She is happy and you get a more jovial partner as compared to when she feels overwhelmed with housework. Imagine if both the man and his female partner return from work at about the same time, and the man goes to put on the TV while the woman rushes to prepare dinner for the family. She is probably stressed out from work already and if she could get some help at this point, even with things like setting the table or giving the kids a bath and putting them to bed, she knows she would only have to focus on dinner and her partner can take care of the other pressing chores for the evening. That evening most likely goes beautifully and you maintain a happy partner.

- **Divide up chores:**

  It is not a question of splitting the housework 50/50 between both of you, but more of sitting together and discussing with your partner about who does what in the house [20]. Ask your partner what you could do for them that would make them feel like you are helping out. It is good to ask because if you inquire from most men, they believe that they are doing a lot of housework as well, so they don't see why their partners feel otherwise. It might be that the help your female partner really needs from you every evening is to put the kids to bed instead of helping out with dinner. That chore is big enough to make her feel like you are both in the game and she is happy. So, ask your partner so they can tell you what they need to be done.

- **Keep a visible reminder of who does what if this is necessary:**

Sit down and draw up the chores required at home on a daily or weekly basis. Write your name against your chores and your partner's name against theirs. Paste it on the fridge or somewhere else that is visible enough so both of you can check with the list often. Include things like making meals, washing dishes, cleaning up the house, washing the toilets, laundry, bathing the kids, taking the kids to school and recreational activities, taking out the bin, mowing the lawn, changing the sheets, walking the dog, washing the car, etc.

- **Be faithful to do your bit:**
Don't forget to come home to make dinner if it is your turn or to take the bin out. Not doing your allotted chores can cause friction in the home, so do your best possible to be involved. Discuss with your partner if for any reason you would want to make changes to your chores and of course let them know if you are running late to make dinner. Communication cannot be overemphasized.

Sex

Sex is a challenging topic and many couples find it rather hard to communicate about it, even though sex can cause such big conflicts in relationships that can leave a person feeling embarrassed, hurt, or rejected. Gottman's opinion of this is that when partners can't seem to talk about their true feelings and needs during sex, then, unfortunately, there is nothing much that can be done [20]. Chances are if you don't speak up, then your partner continues to do what they feel is good for you and you won't get what you really want. How often would you love to have sex? What time of the day would you prefer the most? Where do you want to be touched more? Do you want the foreplay to last longer? These are important sexual issues a couple should talk seriously about to improve their sexual experience and reduce conflicts that can arise. Understanding each other's needs would also deepen your intimacy. Unfortunately, the main reason for sex-related conflicts is the lack of communication. Here are some practical tips that can help avoid and resolve some of these conflicts successfully:

- **Talk about sex in a way that makes you feel comfortable and safe:**

  Talking about sex is perhaps not as easy as it is portrayed in a lot of books these days. It is also different for everyone. One of the reasons why some people don't communicate clearly to their partners on their sexual needs might be because they aren't sure if what they want to ask is appropriate. Would your partner be happy to do what you want, or would they make fun of your request? Another factor is that people can feel very vulnerable with their bodies and wonder if their partner finds them attractive after putting on some extra weight or the birth of a baby. Thirdly, some people wonder if they are actually doing things right and whether their partner sees them as a good lover or not. Honest and clear communication can become withdrawn with some of these factors running through your head. First of all, you need to just relax. Talking about sex should be in the most empathic and gentle manner possible. Be very sensitive to how you communicate your needs to your partner, as they can perceive it differently if your words are harsh, accusing, or full of blame. Sex is very important to growing intimacy in a relationship and you want to feel satisfied and have fun as well. Great sex also brings a feeling of value and acceptance into a relationship. So instead of saying "Take your hand from there" or "No, don't touch me there", why not say "I really love it when you touch me here and here". Don't say "You don't kiss me enough", instead say "I really enjoyed your kiss the last time, can you kiss me more?" You see, words make so much difference.

- **Don't ever perceive your partner as inexperienced or unskillful in lovemaking:** Sex is more than just the physical connection you get with your partner; it is deep intimacy. So, even if you or your partner is new to the game, do not make them feel that way as this can greatly affect their confidence to express themselves. Instead, encourage your partner in love and as they get more comfortable.

- **Always agree on what is comfortable for both of you:**
You should be in agreement about exploring new activities or positions during sex. If your partner wants you to do something and you are not quite comfortable or ready for that activity, you should let them know. There's no need for doing what you don't want to do.

- **Build up sexual desire throughout the day:**
If you want to see your sex life really improve in terms of creating and sustaining your partner's desire to have sex with you, then start to build up each other's desire throughout the day. Sex doesn't have to start at the point where you are ready to take off your clothes in the bedroom. It can start several hours before the actual act is carried out. Pay attention to your partner's sensuality. Give plenty of hugs, caresses, kisses, and holding of

hands. Let your bodies touch as often as you get the opportunity.

These activities start to gradually build up sexual desires in your partner, who might be usually less interested, and the result is an incredible sexual experience later on.

- **Bring in the variety:**
Spice up your sex life with some variety. Be open enough to try out new ways to explore your partner's body and new sexual positions. Sex takes some work as well, and if you keep repeating the military position all the time, chances are one day you or your partner will begin to get bored and wonder what's happening to your intimacy, so spice it up. Take your experience to another level by doing something new that both of you are comfortable with.

- **Share your sexual fantasies with each other:**

Some people have sexual fantasies they dream about trying out with their partner, but are too embarrassed to share it with them. You and your partner should understand each other when it comes to sex. If your partner shares their fantasy of wanting to play pirate during sex, don't laugh at them, even if you don't understand the reason for their fantasy.

Regard it as play and have fun. In the end, it only deepens the bond and intimacy that both of you share.

- **You can learn more about sex:**
  Most people claim to know a thing or two about sex, but do you really understand a man's body or that of a woman? A lot of information you might have accumulated while growing up might not be exactly correct or totally wrong, so be open to learning. There are great resources that you can invest in and learn more about pleasing your partner. Investing in your sexual life is surely a great investment.

- **Master your partner's preferences:**
  Try to remember where you touched your partner the last time that they really loved. Remember their likes and dislikes during sex and use that as an advantage to always keep your sex heightened, giving each other pleasure in the best possible way.

Chapter 8: The Sex Drive - Why Men And Women Are Different And Rituals For Healthy Relationships

The Sex Drive In Men And Women

Men wonder why it takes so much fuss and drama for a woman to have sex – she wants to talk first or take a shower. She wants scented candles or her partner to do the dishes first. She wants the bed made and the lights just perfect. Sometimes, as her partner, you can do all these things for her, then make a wrong statement about her sister and boom – the sex is off – she is no longer interested and her partner just can't understand how her desire can just disappear like that.

Here's the thing, women also wonder how a man can get an erection after a fight an hour ago. Does he just want me for sex? Is that all that matters to him? Why is he in such a hurry? Why does he want sex all the time? I thought we had it yesterday, how can you want sex again? These thoughts tell us clearly that there is such a big difference in the sexual drives of men and women. So, do men actually have a stronger sex drive than women? The answer is a big 'yes' – they do, and we will outline the reasons, but first what is really the science of sex drive?

The sex drive or libido is a person's summed-up desire for sexual activities, which can be influenced by a lot of factors, including psychological, biological, and social elements [3, 12, 26]. The hormone testosterone is the sex drive hormone in the bodies of both men and women. This hormone is also responsible for the development of all the puberty features in men and the production of sperm. It is also responsible for ovulation in women [3, 12, 22].

The production of this hormone can be affected by factors like alcohol consumption, exhaustion, and depleted energy levels. It can also be affected by medical conditions associated with blood sugar levels, blood pressure, and depression. Old or young age (not reaching puberty) can become an affecting factor too in the production of this hormone and of course, we can't forget emotional factors like an unresolved conflict in a relationship [22].

A person's moral, religious, or cultural values can also aid to keep testosterone in check [11, 22] since being sexually attracted to someone doesn't mean you can automatically have sex with the person.

It is very important to understand sex drive since it is such a key factor in starting and maintaining an intimate relationship. A once thriving relationship can become adversely affected when there is a lack or loss of sexual drive in one or both individuals. If these changes remain unresolved, serious conflicts in the relationship might be the end game. Research shows that men have a higher sex drive than women in general [22]. Even though testosterone is present in men and women, it is known to play a much greater role in men [22]. It is no wonder then that a healthy male, fully attaining puberty, has about twenty times the amount of testosterone when compared with a healthy female at puberty [22].

Now that we understand the science behind the sex drive, here are some patterns backed up by research that clearly differentiates the sex drive of men and women:

- **Men want sex more often than women:**
  Research carried out by Roy Baumeister reviewing several men and women, shows that a man's desire for sex can be at different stages in a relationship, meaning it doesn't really depend on whether the relationship is just starting or is at a later stage, men will still want more frequent sex than women. Men are also inclined to having more sexual partners in their lifetime than women [12].

- **Men think more often about sex than women:**

Another research carried out by Lauman showed that most healthy males below the age of 60 think about sex at least once a day [25]. On average, women don't think about sex that often. Baumeister's research also showed that men had more frequent and varied sexual fantasies than women [12].

- **A woman's turn on is more complicated than that of a man:**

Men never seem to understand what exactly turns a woman on, as it varies all the time. The truth is, even women don't fully understand their turn on. For a woman, it is simply more complicated, and a lot of factors can come into play to arousing a woman's sexual desires. Men tend to be more physical – building up sexual desires from what they can see – a powerful form of attraction fueled by their testosterone [22]. It takes more than that for a woman who is more emotional and can be turned on by something as simple as her partner getting her a special gift or even doing some house chores for her.

- **Women are more influenced by socio-cultural and religious factors than men:**
  Baumeister's research also found out that women's willingness to have sex could be influenced by their regular attendance of religious activities as compared to men. Their peer groups or social community can also influence them as well [3, 10, 11].

- **A woman's sexual arousal and satisfaction are not as direct as a man's:**
  When a man wants to have sex, he can literally get into the act and be done with it, but that is so different for a woman who wants some wooing. A typical woman wants to anticipate and build up the longing for sex before it is eventually carried out. It is similar to carrying out a plot in romance novels. Women are more delicate and tend to build up layers of emotion [10]. This is why some women

want to talk before the sexual act begins and her partner can't understand why they are delaying the excitement.

- **Orgasms differ in men and women:**
  Research has shown that a man tends to have far more orgasms than a woman does, and they reach orgasms faster too. A man takes an average of 4 minutes to reach orgasm from his first thrust, but it takes a woman an average of 11 minutes to do so. Also, 75% of men claim to always reach orgasm during sex, while only 26% of women do all the time [11]. It is clear that it is easier for a man to reach orgasm than it is for a woman.

Rituals For Healthy Relationships

We live in a modern world and couples are getting busier by the day. People are involved in full-time careers and the daily pressures of modern life. It is getting quite challenging for the modern-day, high paced couple to keep up with maintaining healthy relationships. Breakups and divorces are on the rise because of unresolvable conflicts that couples simply can't keep up with. It is so much easier to fall in love than to stay in love for a long period of time. If a couple's love is going to stand the test of time, they have to be very conscious and intentional about it. This requires applying intentional approaches to relationships in order to create lasting love. Putting in place simple everyday rituals can help to ensure that your relationship doesn't get lost in this fast-paced world. If you do nothing about it, then your love begins to dry out and you will grow apart without even knowing it.

There are so many rituals talked about by psychologists and relationship experts globally – some are really practicable for a lot of couples while some others can be really abstract or difficult to keep up with. Here I have put together some very practical rituals that can diligently be inculcated into even the busiest lives. Don't forget that there has to be some effort on each person's part as it takes two people to build a successful love relationship.

- **Compliment each other at least once every day:**
  Make it a practice to give compliments every day. It shows that no matter how busy you are, you still take note of the little details on your partner's body and in life in general. So, stop for a second just before you run out that door to say, "You look so nice today", "You look so handsome this morning", "Oh and I love that dress you have on".

- **Establish the same sleep routine as much as possible:**
  Try to go to bed and wake up at the same time. Remember, you have to be intentional about it, so try to plan ahead, except when your work schedules differ of course. Going to bed at the same time leaves you some time to talk and get really intimate with your partner before going off to sleep. Starting your day off with your partner is also a great way of bonding before the rush of the day begins.

- **Eat at least one meal together as a couple:**
  Dinner is usually the most feasible, as most people will be back home in the evening. Decide to eat together, even if you have to wait a little bit for your partner to return. Let dinnertime be a special moment for both of you where you can share about your day and catch up on what's going on in your lives. It is a great opportunity to communicate face to face, so don't miss out on this.

- **Set aside the phones during dinner and at bedtime:**
  These are two key moments where you have a few minutes to talk as a couple. Don't get distracted by the constant buzzing of social media alerts. Set the phone aside for these moments that should mean a lot to you and your partner so you can spend some quality time together and have quality conversations where you can focus on your partner the whole time.

- **Check-in on your partner during the day to find out how their day is going:**

  Keeping communication going throughout the day can be a great way to build and sustain intimacy in relationships. Make a quick call at lunchtime and talk for 5 minutes. You can send texts as well - just keep some communication going and don't wait until you are home in the evening.

- **Make kisses and hugs a tradition:**

  Remember the power of touching [1, 28]. Kiss your partner goodbye before leaving the house and kiss again when you return. Give hugs as well. Don't let your relationship get to a point where you can't even give welcome hugs that take only a second. If you find it hard to give hugs, then this might be a red flag that you are growing apart. You can resume hugs again and hopefully, with other rituals, your intimacy will deepen again.

- **Show appreciation:**

Say "thank you" to your partner when they do something for you, even if they do it for you all the time. It makes them feel loved and appreciated.

- **Don't get too big to apologize:**
Learn to say the magic words "I am sorry", and learn to mean it too. Apologize when you are wrong instead of trying to defend yourself all the time. Sincere apologies work wonders with many, so don't underestimate the power of an apology.

- **Do things together:**
Choose an activity that both of you can do together every day or as often as you can. Some couples exercise together. This is surely a great way of bonding and spending quality time together. You can take walks in the evening together or go to the gym together, cook dinner together or weed the garden together. It doesn't have to be all talk – just spending quality time together with your partner is a great way of deepening intimacy and sharing your feelings.

- **Schedule dates:**

  Plan date night together as frequently as you can. It doesn't have to be going to an elaborate restaurant all the time. It can be a movie night at the cinema or at home with some homemade popcorn! It could be going to watch your favorite sports club play or going to the beach. The point is, if you don't plan ahead by inculcating a date night into your calendars, then there might not be time for these outings. Dates should be special moments for both of you without the distractions of the kids or work and friends. Hold hands – remind yourselves of why you chose each other and feel like you are teenagers in love for the first time again.

- **Don't forget to say the words "I love you":**

  We could get so used to saying these words that they start to mean less and less to us, but some people need to hear you say it, so why not? Say it to your partner as frequently as you can and try to mean it too.

A Final Note

If you have read through the pages of this book and have come to this point, then allow me to commend you on doing such a great thing for yourself and for your relationship.

Whether you are looking to spice up your relationship or revive it completely, I hope that you can apply some of the strategies here to reach your expectations. Remember that creating a lasting, flaming, love relationship takes hard work from two determined and loving people, which has to be continuous. If you stop working at your relationship, then the results you enjoy will start to fade gradually, so please don't stop.

Begin getting to really know your partner and understand the primary way they feel loved. A huge part of this book has focused on communication because it holds an essential key to growing love relationships and intimacy, so work on your communication skills by asking kind, open-ended questions. Practice your active listening and safe conversation techniques too at every given opportunity. These practical strategies will help resolve conflicts more easily and effectively; they will also help tackle the typical solvable problems like stress and others mentioned here.

The world is moving at such a fast pace, but it doesn't have to take our relationships with it. We can take charge of our lives and channel it the way we want it to go, refusing to let all the stress and smartphones control us. We are in control of our world and we have chosen to share our journey with wonderful people who love us. Let's make it count. Love doesn't have to fade away after a few months or a few years – let our love be that which lasts a lifetime or two.

References

1. Abraira, VE and Ginty, DD 20, 'The Sensory Neurons of Touch', Neuron, vol. 79, no. 4 pp10 – 101.

2. Amato, PR 2010, 'Research on Divorce: Continuing Trends and New Developments'. Journal of Marriage and Family, vol. 72, no. 3, pp. 650–666.

3. Anders, SM, Steiger, J and Goldeyd, KL 2015, 'Effects of gendered behaviour on testosterone in women and men', Proc Natl Acad Sci, vol. 112, no. 45, pp. 13805–13810.

4. Apter, T 2010, What Do You Want From Me? Learning How To Get Along With The In-Laws, Norton, New York.

5. Apter, T 2018, Passing Judgment: Praise And Blame In Everyday Life, Norton, New York.

6. Ardiel, EL and Rankin, CH 2010, 'The importance of touch in development', Paediatr Child Health, vol. 15, no. 3, pp. 153–156.

7. Aron Arthur et al 1996, 'The experimental generation of interpersonal closeness: a procedure and some preliminary findings'. SAGE social science collection, pp. 363 – 377.

8. Barbach, L and Geisinger, D 1993, Going the distance: finding and keeping livelong love, Plume, New York.

9. Boehm, J K, and Lyubomirsky, S 2008, 'Does happiness promote career success?' Journal of Career Assessment, vol. 16, no. 1, pp. 101–116.

10. Baumeister, RF 2000, 'Gender Differences in Erotic Plasticity: The Female Sex Drive as Socially Flexible and Responsive'. Psychological Bulletin, vol. 126, no. 3, pp. 347-374.

11. Baumeister, RF 2004, 'Gender and erotic plasticity: sociocultural influences on the sex drive', Sexual and Relationship Therapy, vol. 19, no. 2, pp. 1468bp-1479.

12. Baumeister, RF, Catanese, KR and Vohs, KD 2001, 'Is There a Gender Difference in Strength of Sex Drive? Theoretical Views, Conceptual Distinctions, and a Review of Relevant Evidence', Personality and Social Psychology, Vol. 5, No. 3, pp. 242–273.

13. Bellezza, S, Paharia, N and Keinan, A 2017 Conspicuous Consumption of Time: When Busyness and Lack of Leisure Time Become a Status Symbol, Journal of Consumer Research, vol. 44, no. 1, pp. 118–138.

14. Chapman, G 2015, The Five Love Languages: The Secret To Love That Lasts, Moody Press, U.S.

15. Dasgupta, PB 2017, Detection And Analysis Of Human Emotions Through Voice And Speech

Pattern Processing, International Journal Of Computer Trends And Technology, vol 152, no 1, pp 1-3.

16. Doell, F 2003, Partners' Listening Style And Relationship Satisfaction: Listening To Understand Vs Listening To Respond. Graduate thesis. The University of Toronto Psychology Department.

17. Drago, E 2015, 'The Effect Of Technology On Face-Face Communication', Elton Journal Of Undergraduate Research In Communications, vol. 6, no. 1, pp. 1 – 2.

18. Elsobeihi, MM, Abu-Nasir, SS 2017, 'Effects Of Mobile Technology On Human Relationships', International Journal Of Engineering And Information Systems, vol. 5, no. 5, pp. 110 – 125.

19. Fisher, H 2004, Why We Love – the Nature and Chemistry of Romantic Love, Henry Holt and Company, New York.

20. Gottman, J 2015, The Seven Principles For Making Marriage Work, Harmony, New York.

21. Gottman, J 2002, The Relationship Cure, Harmony, New York.

22. Goymann, W and Wingfield, JC 2014, 'Male-to-female testosterone ratios, dimorphism, and life history—what does it really tell us?' Behavioural Ecology, Vol. 25, no. 4, pp. 685–699.

23. Hartman, T, 1999, The Colour Code: A New Way To See Yourself, Your Relationship And Life, Scribner, New York.

24. Hertlein, K 2008, 'Technology, relationships and problems: a research synthesis', Journal of marital and family therapy, vol. 34, no. 4, pp. 445 – 60.

25. Laumann, EO, Gagnon, JH, Michael, RT, and Michaels, S 1994, The Social Organization of Sexuality, University of Chicago Press, Chicago.

26. Money, J 1986, Lovemaps: Clinical Concepts of Sexual/Erotic Health and Pathology, Paraphilia, and Gender Transposition in Childhood, Adolescence, and Maturity, Irvington, New York.

27. Nasir, JM 2015, Still Together? The Role Of Acoustic Features In Predicting Marital Outcome, Interspeech, vol 2015, pp 2499 – 2503.

28. Rose JK, Sangha S, Rai S, Norman KR and Rankin CH 2005, 'Decreased sensory stimulation reduces behavioural responding, retards development, and alters neuronal connectivity in Caenorhabditis elegans', J Neurosci, vol. 25, no. 31, pp. 7159-68.

29. Schuman, H and Presser, S 1979, The Open and Closed Question, American Sociological Review, vol.44, no. 5, pp. 692-712.

30. Schwartz RS and Olds J 2001, 'Ebb and flow: a theory of lasting relationships', Harvard Rev Psychiatry, vol. 9, no. 10, pp. 189-196.

31. Singer, E and Couper, MP, 2017, Some Methodological Uses of Responses to Open Questions and Other Verbatim Comments in Quantitative Surveys, Methods, Data, Analyses, Vol. 11, no. 2, pp. 115-134.

32. Stoufer, T 2013, The Everything Budgeting Book: Practical Advise For Saving And Managing Your Money – From Daily Budgets To Long Term Goals. Available from: Ebook Library [May 5, 2019].

33. Tennov, D 2005, A Scientist Looks at Romantic Love and Calls It "Limerence": The Collected Works of Dorothy Tennov, Greenwich, CT: The Great American Publishing Society (GRAMPS), USA.

34. Walker, F, and Gibson, J, 2011, the art of active listening: how to double your communication skills in 30 days. Available from: Ebook Library, [May 12, 2019].

35. Wood, A and John, B K, The Surprising Power of Questions. From the May–June 2018 issue. Harvard business review.

Disclaimer

The information contained in this book and its components is meant to serve as a comprehensive collection of strategies that the author of this book has done research about. Summaries, strategies, tips, and tricks are only recommendations by the author, and reading this book will not guarantee that one's results will exactly mirror the author's results.

The author of this book has made all reasonable efforts to provide current and accurate information for the readers of this book. The author and its associates will not be held liable for any unintentional errors or omissions that may be found.

The material in the book may include information by third parties. Third party materials are comprised of opinions expressed by their owners. As such, the author of this book does not assume responsibility or liability for any third party material or opinions.

The publication of third party material does not constitute the author's guarantee of any information, products, services, or opinions contained within third party material. Use of third party material does not guarantee that your results will mirror our results. Publication of such third party material is simply a recommendation and expression of the author's own opinion of that material.

Whether because of the progression of the Internet, or the unforeseen changes in company policy and editorial submission guidelines, what is stated as fact at the time of this writing may become outdated or inapplicable later.

written expressed and signed permission from the author.

Printed by BoD™in Norderstedt, Germany